This is Basildon

This is Basildon

Michael Healy

Copyright © 2009 Michael Healy

The moral right of the author has been asserted.

Apart from any fair dealing for the purposes of research or private study, or criticism or review, as permitted under the Copyright, Designs and Patents Act 1988, this publication may only be reproduced, stored or transmitted, in any form or by any means, with the prior permission in writing of the publishers, or in the case of reprographic reproduction in accordance with the terms of licences issued by the Copyright Licensing Agency. Enquiries concerning reproduction outside those terms should be sent to the publishers.

Matador
5 Weir Road
Kibworth Beauchamp
Leicester LE8 0LQ, UK
Tel: (+44) 116 279 2299
Fax: 0116 279 2277
Email: books@troubador.co.uk
Web: www.troubador.co.uk/matador

ISBN 978 1848762 541

British Library Cataloguing in Publication Data.
A catalogue record for this book is available from the British Library.

Typeset in 11pt Goudy Old Style by Troubador Publishing Ltd, Leicester, UK

Matador is an imprint of Troubador Publishing Ltd

Printed in Great Britain by the MPG Books Group, Bodmin and King's Lynn

To Patsy Connolly

Acknowledgements

I would like to thank my family, who helped out in many ways throughout the making of this book.

Special mention to - Mikey Cartwright www.ponderosa.org for his assistance with the clubs, groups and societies of Basildon

Many thanks to the following people, who in one way or another helped me in the making of this book.....
Evening Echo, Basildon District Council, Essex Records Office, William Corriger, Lin Alexandre, Benjamin Levy, Deborah Nomed, Reinhard Schneider, Nana Woywod, Volker Sternemann, Christian Specht, Anthony O'Connor (Big Ant), Louisa Stevenson-Hamilton, George Bell, Richard Mann, Scott Fairbrass, Dan Bulter, Bob Ayres, Frank McLeod, Brain Waterman, Wayne Morgan, Peter King, Louise Pike, Eike Mangold, Kira Lewis, Aishatu Shuaibu, Betty Jeffery, Colin Jeffery, Adam Fontain, Peter Murton, Andrew Wood, Tony Palmer, Craig Brittney, Ashley Christopher Faiers, Scott Smallman, Karen Barton, Trevor Bavin, Matthew Hollingshead, Merlyn Buckley, Joyce Farrow, John Spriggs, Len Stanway, David Church, Charlie Meads, Geoff Miller, Jamie Rogers, Emma Rowell, John Swinbank, Wayne Hunt, Julia Tennant, Kevin Green, Wendy Taylor, Steve Henaman, Gyp Kenton-Romay, Andrew Walsh, Steven Bowler, Lousie Annis-Rodgers, Frank Doyle, Richard Haywood, Nicolas Mingy, Kate Boucher, Stephen Waters, Anita Bryant, Grant Tony Lee Richards, Connor Mulvey, Michael Murnane, Derek Brooker, Cathie Brock, Tony Dow.

For nearly helping me, I'd like to thank Kimberly Harding, Gareth Biggs and Kevin Green.

Also, for absolutely no reason at all, I like to acknowledge the following people: Danny Barry, Ryan Neale, Carl Rodgers, Stuart Lambert, Danielle Nolan, Anthony O'Connor (little Ant), Rory O'Brien, Wesley Barton, James Greenan, Stewart Haywood, Kate Ramsey, Michael Walsh, Jacob Chilton, Jack Wilkins, Joe Wilkins, Bradley Paynter, Dennis Rogers, Peter Cumming, Rebecca Iley, Darren Rogers
and David Lambert.

Photo Acknowledgments

All photographs were taken by the author with the exception of the following...
Mikey Cartwright - www.ponderosa.org page 73 (top) and 80
Steve Engelmayer - 105
Andrea Elisii - 146, 148
Jamie Rogers - 163
Roger M. P. - http://livepict.com - 154 and 160
Wendy Taylor - 134, 136
Eric Hardy - 106
Mark Toner - 105

Every effort has been made to trace ownership of photographs and to check that the facts given in this book are correct. My apologies for any unwitting errors or omissions.

Foreword

Our 60 year anniversary is a good place to start for a book about the history of Basildon and its people. I first moved to Basildon at just 9 years old and I can remember the excitement of getting our first family house, having lived in a flat above a shop in east London. I moved to Pitsea, went to Pitsea Juniors and then Chalvedon school and quickly felt at home in my new community, despite my sadness at leaving my friends. I never dreamed that this town that I had made my home would one day make me its Member of Parliament.

I have good memories of those early days. Where Pitsea Market and the shops now stand there was a pony field (which we would only rarely cross, feeling safer walking round it) and a lane leading down to the 'Tudor Mansions' shops and cinema. I can remember going as a family to Carry on Camping – and I still love the silliness of Carry On films!

On Saturday mornings Mum would take us along to the Towngate in Basildon (the old Towngate, the site now being part of the Westgate Shopping Centre) where we would have fun trying to make something on the potter's wheel or take part in some of the many other activities for young people, while she shopped.

What differentiates this from other history books about the district is the community section and the information on the individuals from our local groups and societies. As the Member of Parliament I never cease to be impressed by those that run and get involved in local groups and societies – and have great fun doing so. I have been roundly thrashed at table tennis by members of the Basildon Disabled Sports Club – they showed me no mercy as they took point after point!

For many of us this history is also a snapshot of parts of our life – and you will enjoy reading it all the more because of that.

Angela Smith MP (Basildon & East Thurrock)
July 2009

History

This chapter covers the many fascinating periods throughout the area's existence. With references to times dating back as far as the Bronze Age, Iron Age, Romans, Anglo-Saxons, and Medieval Britain. We then follow with a more detailed look at the modern era - the settlement of the Plotlanders, World War II and the creation and development of the 'Basildon Newtown'.

The story of how Basildon came to be has been covered many times before. This section of the book only includes what I personally consider to be the most interesting and relevant details of the towns' history. If you want to learn even more about the subject, I recommend you refer to the bibliography page for suggestions of further reading.

Early History of Basildon

Basildon may only be 60 years old, but the villages and towns that make up the district have a history which can be traced back thousands of years.

Starting with the Pre Historic era, there has been evidence found locally which dates back as far as the Bronze Age. Through archaeological findings we have been able to discover a little about the people who lived here during that time.

Items were found during the construction of Swan Mead School (now Cherry Tree Primary). Fragments of Bronze weapons said to date between 800 – 700BC were found by builders laying the foundations for the school. 'The Vange Hoard', can now be seen at the Southend Museum on Victoria Avenue.

A Bronze Age axe was also found, 6 feet below ground, at Merrick Marshes, Vange (nr Marsh Farm) when builders were installing some brick making machinery.

Excavations on settlements dating back to the Iron Age have been carried out in Wickford, Billericay, Langdon Hills, Basildon, and also Ramsden which is said to have been continually occupied from 550-150 BC.

The Romans invaded in 43AD and with them came civilisation as we now know it. They built roads, towns and effectively made Britain into the power it is today. A known Roman road passes Basildon at nearby Brentwood and there have been findings of Roman artefacts in Billericay, Wickford and Vange.

At a field near Vange Hall (at the junction of Puck Lane and Clay Hill Road) there were several Roman tiles and bricks found. In Wickford, excavations at Beauchamp's Farm uncovered nearly 200 coins, pottery, and metal work. all dating back to the time of Roman occupancy in the country. Roman coins and pottery were also discovered at Blunts Wall, Billericay dating between AD69 and AD636, it is also reported that there was once a Roman Fort there, although unfortunately no trace of the site can be seen today as it was completely destroyed by the Saxons during their invasion.

The Anglo Saxons were next to settle on these shores and many reminders of their existence remains today both in and around Basildon. The word Essex derives from 'East Seaxe' or 'East Saxon' and many of the place names in the local area also have Saxon origins. The first King of Essex, Serbert, is reported to have lived at Burstead, and included London (which at the time was in ruin) as part of his kingdom.

In 1066 at the Battle of Hastings, Harold II is killed after being hit by an arrow in the eye. The Norman invaders lead by William the Conqueror, soon bring the country under Norman rule, taking us into Medieval Britain. A survey of the country was held by order of William I and its findings were given the title of the Domesday Book which was completed in 1086.

Three manors of Basildon were mentioned in the book under the heading of 'Hundred of Barstable' they were Belesdunam, Berlesduna, and Berdestapla.

The manor of Berlesduna (thought to be a variation on the spelling of Beorhtel's Hill / Basildon) was held by a Norman landowner called Sven the Sheriff. He was also known as 'Sven of Essex' and resided at Rayleigh Castle.

Belesdunam (another variation of the word Basildon) was held by Turold, renowned for being the most ruthless of all Norman landlords at that time. His image was recorded on the Bayern Tapestry, which is on display at the Bayeux Museum in Normandy, France.

The manor of Berdestapla (thought be a variation of the spelling of Barstable) was held by Odo, the Bishop of Bayeux. Odo, the half brother of William the Conqueror, was later incarcerated after a being found guilty in plotting to kill the Pope.

Medieval England experienced quite a few revolts, but the most memorable being the Peasants' Revolt of 1381. Demanding that they receive higher wages and better working conditions, the peasants marched from Essex and Kent onto London lead by Wat Tyler. The revolt managed to capture the Tower of London, something which had never been done before, or since. Wat Tyler was killed during the revolt and everything went back to the way it was before, however the unpopular Poll Tax was abolished and wages did subsequently rise, but this may have been due to other factors and not necessarily as a result of their revolt. In the 1980s Wat Tyler Country Park in Pitsea was named in honor of the revolutionary leader.

Start of the New Town

It has been 60 years since Basildon was declared as being the location for the latest 'New Town' and there were many factors which lead to its creation.

The New Towns Act (1946) was introduced to house the high number of people who lost their homes as a result of the bombings during WWII. There were however some New Towns which were built solely to improve already existing areas.

Stevenage in Hertfordshire was designated as the first of the 'New Towns' on the 1st August 1946.

There have since been several more built in England including Bracknell, Chorley, Corby, Crawley, Harlow, Hatfield, Hemel Hempstead, Leyland, Milton Keynes, Northampton, Peterborough, Preston, Redditch, Runcorn, Skelmersdale, Telford, Warrington, Washington and Welwyn Garden City.

The story of how Basildon came to be a New Town starts with the introduction of the Bank Holidays Act 1871 which gave workers in London the opportunity to take day trips.

In 1888 the LTS (London, Tilbury, Southend Railway Company) built a direct line from Barking to Pitsea, added a new station at Laindon and turned Pitsea station into a junction for both the new line and the existing line which diverted via Tilbury.

Laindon & Pitsea were both predominantly agricultural areas but poor harvests in the late 1870's left farmers having to sell the land to property developers. The land was broken down into small plots (approx. 7m x 53m) and sold at auction to Londoners looking to realise their dreams of owning a place in the countryside.

Small basic housing was built on these plots and used by owners as 'weekend retreats'. Most were not connected to water mains, electricity or gas and the roads were nothing more than dirt tracks, which in bad weather would be almost unusable. However the lack of amenities and luxury was considered a minor sacrifice as it allowed them to escape the hustle and bustle of the polluted city, breathe clean air and grow their own fresh fruit and vegetables.

During WWII many considered living permanently at their weekend homes. The basic living conditions of the plotland settlements appearing more favourable than the constant threat of air raids in the city. Some feared that if they stayed in London their families would be split up, if children were required to be evacuated.

After the war had ended many chose not to return to their homes in London, having grown accustomed to the country lifestyle. Billericay Council, who at the time were responsible for the area, were left with the major task of improving the living conditions of what was described by councillors as being 'rural slums'. However they did not have the funds for such a major operation so approached the government for assistance. The government were facing a problem of their own; there were tens of thousands of people from East and West Ham who were without homes after the area suffered badly at the hands of German bombs. The solution was to build a New Town at a site proposed between the villages of Pitsea and Laindon thus solving both problems.

The name given to the New Town, Basildon, was taken from the very small village of the same name which existed roughly near the centre of the proposed location.

On the 4th of January 1949, Basildon was officially designated as a New Town and the Basildon Development Corporation (BDC) was formed shortly after. The first task of the BDC was to buy up existing properties in the area to make way for the planned building work to commence. Those residents not willing to accept the offers made by the BDC were issued Compulsory Purchase Orders - a legality which allows authorities to obtain land without the owners consent.

Naturally, many residents were unhappy with the proposed plans and it was the job of The Labour MP and Minister of Town and Country Planning, Lewis Silkin, to convince people that the creation of the New Town was in fact a good thing and that it would benefit the people of the area.

In front of a hostile crowd at the Laindon High Road School in September 1948, Silkin made his speech *"Basildon will become a city which people all over the world will want to visit. It will be a place where all classes of community can meet freely together on equal terms and enjoy common cultural recreational facilities"* The local people were unconvinced and the RPA (Residential Protection Association) was formed to oppose the plan. Needless to say their efforts were unsuccessful and the plan to build the town went ahead.

First New House of the New Town

The first New Town house to be occupied in Basildon was 61 Redgrave Road, Vange. In June 1951 Betty and John Walker, with their two children John, aged 6, and Valerie, 15 months old became the first residents of the New Town.

The family had spent the previous 4 years on the housing list in London's East Ham, so the prospect of their own place in Basildon was like a dream come true.

Shortly after the move, the family played host to an official welcoming party. The guest list included Lady Whitmore (wife of Lord Lieutenant of Essex) and the Major's of both East and West Ham. The Walkers recall the paint in the upstairs rooms still being wet and how a team of gardeners had been round the day before to lay turf and decorate the back yard with an assortment of plants and flowers.

The Walkers were extremely happy with the move. It was the first self contained unit the family had lived in, after many years in shared accommodation.

They were especially happy with the garden, as it allowed them to grow vegetables. The whole area had a countryside feel to it and this was something the Walkers very much appreciated.

The roads had been built but the pavements had yet to be completed,

The first house of the new town

so mud was a major factor in early Basildon New Town life. The nearest shop was approximately 1 mile away, a grocers and post office combined close to the Barge Public House.

The Walkers were victims to a burglary just one year after moving to Basildon. A design fault on the front doors meant that a person with small hands and arms could reach in the letter box and open the latch. The thieves took the Walkers television and carpet. These burglaries were common place during the first couple of years in Redgrave Road. Eventually the council installed iron bars to the insides of the letter boxes which put a stop to the break-ins, but would occasionally cause damage to letters and parcels pushed through the door.

In 1956, just five years after coming to Basildon, the Walkers relocated to Australia. They returned to Essex in the 60's with the family moving into a house on Canvey Island.

Eric and Marjorie Hawkridge, along with their three children, became the Walkers first neighbours at No.63. They themselves were followed by the Bartlett's at No.59 and in August 1951 the Martin family became the fourth residents of the New Town.

Phyllis Martin described the experience as like "moving into paradise" Having come from Custom House, Canning Town and living in a modest two bedroom building which had no hot water, a galvanised bath and an outside toilet. The move to a house with not only a separate bathroom but a garden as well was just great. At the time of moving in, the gardens were just big piles of clay, however it was still better than having no garden at all!

First School in the New Town

Once the new houses had been built and families started to move into the town, it became quite apparent that a new school was needed to take some of the strain from the already existing ones in the area. In 1954 Swan Mead School became the first to open in Basildon New Town.

Swan Mead was built as temporary school to "fill a need" and the idea was for it, at a later date, to be either replaced by a permanent school or removed altogether. It was to act as an overspill for the other overcrowded schools in the area.

In the first week the school took in 95 new pupils, 85 of which coming from the same school.

The first Head Teachers of the Swan Mead Junior & Infants schools were Mr Goodfellow and Mrs Davis.

Junior School Headmaster – Mr Bernard Goodfellow

Mr Goodfellow became a teacher in 1939, three days before the outbreak of the war. His first job was with a school in Dagenham and his first task as a teacher was to assist in the evacuation of the children to Suffolk. For nearly 5 weeks he was looking after hundreds of children, without assistance, at a location out near Saxmundham, Suffolk. There he had to cook, clean and generally look after all of the children. Talk about being thrown in at the deep end!

Swan Mead School was Mr Goodfellow's first Head teacher position. His employment was due to start on January 1st 1954, but it wasn't until the 27th April that he officially took the role, as the building work was very much behind schedule. Even after the school had opened there was still a lot of construction work to be done, the gym wasn't finished and the canteen hadn't even been started. The infant school was just foundations so for the early days both Junior and Infant schools shared the one building. The junior's on the top floor, infant's below on the ground.

Mr Goodfellow described the majority of the children as being *"well behaved and well dressed"*.

Infant Head Mistress – Mrs Davis

Mrs Davis's first school was the Pitsea School (now The Len Wastell Infant School) back in 1931. Before getting the job at Swan Mead she was working in a village school in Paglesham, on the outskirts of Rochford.

Mrs Davis was very pleased with the appointment as her husband was already working in Basildon. She looked forward to returning to the district in which she first started her career over 20 years previous. The pupils she taught at Pitsea School would now be of parent age and some of their children may end up being taught by Mrs Davis at Swan Mead School.

She described teaching in Basildon as a challenge, especially for those who had come from areas with more culture, something she claims was seriously lacking in the New Town.

The school has had a long history of break-ins and arson attacks since it opened in 1954. This forced the school to invest in a top of the range security system to protect the building and its contents.

In 2001 the school changed its name from Swan Mead to Cherry Tree Primary School. The school also joined together its separate infant and junior school, combining the two to make one complete building.

On the 1st Anniversary of Swan Mead School, the children contributed to the buying of a Weeping Willow tree which was planted outside of the school.

On the 10th Anniversary the school was open for view for a whole week with concerts and displays of works put on for visitors, including some local dignitaries.

On the 25th Anniversary, the children were treated to a performance of The Mysterious Dr Moffett by the Palace Theatre Travelling Players.

On the 50th 'Golden' Anniversary, a week worth of special events was arranged for the pupils and their parents. There were games, music and prizes and also a visit from author, Anthony Lishau.

First Shop Opened in Town Centre

The first shop to open was Henbest and Sons, a tailor's which relocated from the High Road in Laindon to 65-67 Market Square in the town centre.

Over the years the site has been home to H.Wickisons, a menswear and suit hire shop and DER, a domestic TV rentals outlet. Now the unit is occupied by Robins Pie and Mash Shop.

Pie and Mash is a traditional London working class food. When the people of East London relocated to Basildon they bought with them their love of this Cockney dish.

Mince beef pie and mash potato covered in a parsley sauce called liquor.

Traditionally the only other thing found on the menu of a pie and mash shop would be jellied eels, which are customarily served with vinegar.

History of Pie and Mash

East and South London were populated largely by the working classes. Money was tight so lavish meals using expensive ingredients was not an option.

First shop in the new town

There wasn't much that could survive in The River Thames' murky waters. One such creature which thrived however was the eel, and when boiled in gelatine was not only tasty but would cost very little to make.

Potatoes were also pretty inexpensive and when put together with pies, made solely from cheap mince, and topped with a parsley sauce for flavour, you have yourself a meal.

Goddard's Pie shop is the longest running, being founded in 1890. It was relocated from Deptford and can now be found in Greenwich, London.

There is a tradition for authentic pie and mash shops to be family run, with the recipe for the liquor, a closely guarded secret, being passed down from generation to generation.

Other ... New Town Firsts

- First child born of the New Town was Derek Hood, who lived at 33 Redgrave Road with his parents and sister Valerie. He attended Swan Mead School followed by Woodlands School. The fact that he was the first child born into the town was not discovered until 10 years after his birth, when a Mr Sheppard revealed the news to the family and awarded Derek with an assortment of football gear as a prize.

- The Crane Public house was the New Town's first, built in 1954 on Deny's Drive. George Walker and his wife were the first landlords for the Whitbread & Co. Brewery pub.

- First Factory was built for SE Essex Wholesale Dairies at the Nevendon Industrial Estate – First foundation stone laid by Francis Whitmore. The boss of the company was well known dairyman Charles "Charlie" Markham, he smoked a huge pipe and frequented the Essex Country Club (later known as the Irish Club).

- First pantry shop – Pendle drive – a co-op general store, managed by

Alf Dove, who later became the treasurer of local tenants association and then as Basildon's longest serving District Councillor.

- The first MP for Basildon New Town was Sir Bernard Braine with the Conservative party peer holding the seat from 1950 to 1955.

- The first train from Basildon Train Station was the 4:45am to Fenchurch Street on Monday 25th November 1974.

- Fryerns Baptist Church, Whitmore Way was the first 'New Town' church to be opened on the 3rd July 1954.

- First new road was Eastmayne, a feeder road going from the Southend Artiriel road into the Nevendon industrial estate

- In 1966, Basildon born Graham Bonney (nee Bradley), became the towns' first 'pop star' with the release of his single "Supergirl" reaching no.19 in the UK charts. Graham lived on the Fryerns Estate, before moving to Germany, where he continues to have commercial success as a musician.

Basildon at War

This may come as a surprise to some, but the areas which make up Basildon played witness to its fair share of action during World War II.

German pilots would follow the River Thames, The railway line (LTS) and the roads (A127 and A13) towards London. Some would drop bombs as they pass, others were intercepted in the skies above the town by allied fighter planes based at Hornchurch.

Local historian and author, Peter Lucas, talks in detail about the war years in his three books - Basildon: Behind the Headlines, Basildon - Birth of a City and Basildon (a History of). He includes the following interesting and surprising statistics taken from records kept by an organisation called the ARP (Air Raid Precautions).

During WWII, and within the area of what is now Basildon, a total of 24 people were killed as a result of enemy action, 92 were seriously injured with 454 slightly injured, 149 homes were destroyed and 6,100 damaged.

941 high explosives, 17,400 incendiaries, 48 oil bombs, 18 flying bombs (V1s), 39 rockets (V2s), 28 parachute mines, 10 anti-personnel bombs and 39 phosphorous bombs all fell in the area, as well as 9 German and 17 allied planes crashing within the boundaries of Basildon during that time.

The first bombs to hit were on August 30th 1940 in Gardiners Lane, damaging four cottages and bursting gas and water mains. The last fell in Rectory Road, Pitsea on March 16th 1945.

It is hard to believe, especially to those generations born after the war years, that the sound of air raid sirens, the glare of search lights and the noise of anti aircraft guns were once common place in this area.

At the top of Langdon Hills was the Hutted Camp (now Bentley Farm). This was once a Working Camp for German Prisoners of War (POWs) with the prisoners working on local farms. In return for cheap labour they were given relative freedom around the town, something which caused resentment amongst some of the locals. However, some POWs were accepted and many forged friendships with the local people, some even entered into relationships lasting long after the war had ended.

The GHQ, General Headquarters Line, was a barrier designed to slow down what, in 1940, was seen as an imminent threat of invasion from the Germans. In total there were 4 major 'stop lines' which passed through Essex. The GHQ, which passed through the district of Basildon, started in Somerset then came east as far as Canvey Island before heading north and ending in Yorkshire.

Natural barriers such as rivers, woods and marshes were used as a way of preventing the German troops of advancing, were they to ever land on these shores. Where natural resources were not available, anti-tank ditches were made.

The GHQ line was watched by the Home Guard - an army made up of those who were either too young or too old to already be a part of the forces fighting overseas. Also those who had jobs and skills which required them to stay in England, such as farmers and doctors, were also included.

Across the GHQ line, concrete pill boxes were built, a total of 28,000 throughout the country. Although most have since been demolished, there remains a few in Basildon which managed to survive. In Wat Tyler Park there are four intact pill boxes, as well as others which can be found at various locations throughout the district.

Pill box in Wat Tyler Park

War Memorials

Pitsea, (Howard's Park, off Rectory Road)

A sculpture of a Greek maiden holding what was once a fully operational gas light torch. This memorial was originally located outside the Railway pub before the current roundabout system was built.

Donated by Harold Howard in 1922 it can now be found in the nearby park named in his honour.

Laindon, (High Road, Laindon Shopping Centre)

This 11 ft high black marble column commemorates both WWI and WWII. In 1935 it was erected outside the British Legion Hall (near the site of Laindon High Road School) It was moved to the High Road by Laindon Shopping Centre which has since been subject to major refurbishments and now the memorial is waiting to be relocated.

Wickford, (Runwell Road Gate, Wickford Memorial Park)

These two inscribed tablets were originally located in a Wickford nursing

Pitsea war memorial

home which in 1976 was demolished to make way for a new road. They can now be found by the gates of Wickford Memorial Park. In addition to the stones is the 'Avenue of Remembrance' where there are 59 trees, each accompanied by a plinth and a plaque dedicated to the Wickford residents that died during WWII.

Billericay, (junction of Chapel Street and High Street)

Beside the St Mary Magdalene Church and next to the Chequers Pub, this memorial is dedicated to those who lost their lives during both world wars. Inscribed with the names of the dead as well as a verse from the Gospel of St. John "GREATER LOVE HATH NO MAN THAN THIS"

Laindon war memorial

Wickford war memorial

Little Burstead, (Village green)

This monument is located at the village green on the junction of Rectory Rd, Clock House Rd and Laindon Common Rd. Inscribed with the words:

"Sacred to the memory of the men of Little Burstead who made the supreme sacrifice in the two world wars that we might live in peace and freedom their names will live on forever"

Vange, (St Chads Church, Clay Hill Road)

On the site of what is now Marsh View Court was once Paynters Hill and the previous location for the Vange Memorial. It has since been

Billericay war memorial

Little Burstead war memorial

moved to the grass area in front of St Chads Church on Clay Hill Road. The monument is in honour of those who lost their lives in Great War (aka WWI) of 1914 – 1919.

St Chads War Memorial

Basildon War Memorial

Basildon, (St Martins Church, Town Centre)

Simply inscribed with the words "We will remember them" this memorial can be found by the side of the church entrance in "Gods Garden".

Remembrance Sunday

Each year on Remembrance Sunday the British Legion organise marches throughout the district lead by the ex-servicemen of the area. In 2008 services were held in Basildon, Billericay, Laindon, Pitsea and Wickford. The Basildon march started in the town centre, at Toys-R-Us, with the ex-service men, army cadets, sea cadets and boy scouts making their way towards St Martins Church. A service was held in the church, followed by a two minute silence, before the traditional laying of the wreaths beside the Basildon memorial.

Remembrance Sunday

Basildon District

The Basildon District was established in 1974. It has an overall population of 165.661 (taken from 2001 census) and spans an area of 27,199 acres (42.50 square miles) making it is the largest district in the county.

The District includes Basildon, Laindon, Langdon Hills, Pitsea, Vange, Bowers Gifford, Billericay, Great Burstead, Little Burstead, Ramsden Bellhouse, Crays Hill, North Benfleet and Wickford.

Basildon – Derived from 'Beorthel's Hill'. The name is taken from the ancient family, the Beorthel's. They were thought to have lived in the area pre-364AD. In the 1086 Domesday Book, the town is recorded as 'Berlesduna' and 'Belesdunam'. Over time the name has evolved into Basildon (with the prefix 'don' meaning 'hill')

Laindon – Taken from the River Lyge or Lige, which springs from the hill upon which St Nicholas Church stands. The town is referred to in the Domesday Book as 'Legunduna' and 'Leienduna'

Langdon Hills – The name is broken up into 'Lang' being the Saxon word for 'Long' and 'don' meaning 'upon a hill'. So technically when saying Langdon Hills you are actually saying "Long Hill - Hills"

Welcome to Vange

Pitsea - A Saxon word meaning 'island' or 'marshland of pic'. Recorded in the Domesday Book as 'Piceseia'

Vange – In the Saxon language 'Van' meant a 'fen' or 'marsh' and the prefix 'ge' was said to mean 'district'. In the Domesday Book it is recorded as 'Phenge'.

Bowers Gifford – The name was given by Sir John Gifford, who fought in the Battle of Crécy, one of the most important battles of the Hundred Years' War, back in 1346.

Billericay – No satisfactory Etymology (the study of the sources and development of words) can be suggested for the origin of Billericay. However, some theories suggest that it may have come from the Celtic word for 'Bell' being latinised during the Roman occupancy of Britian.

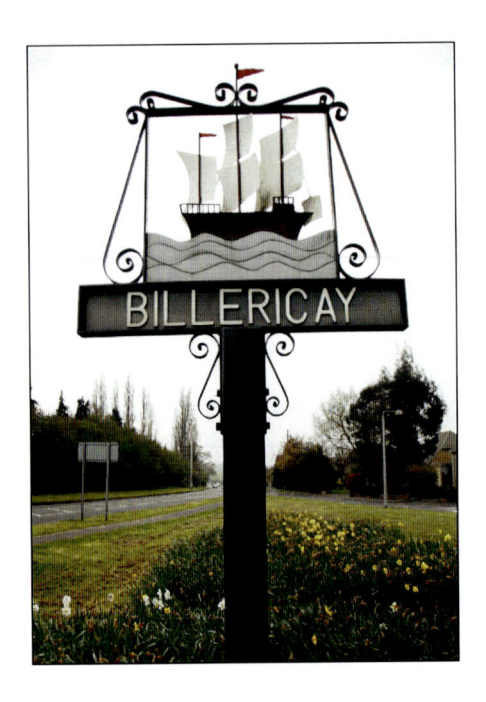

Billericay sign

Great Burstead & Little Burstead – First recorded in c.975 as Burgestede, and referred to in the Domesday Book as Burgesteda A Saxon word meaning a 'fortified place' or 'stronghold'

Ramsden Bellhouse – Ramsden means 'valley where wild garlic grows' and Bellhouse is taken from the ancient family name 'de Belhus'. The Domesday Book recorded the village as Ramesduna.

Crays Hill – Named after Simon De Creye (a knight of Edward I) who took ownership of the manor from Andrew de Blund in 1257.

North Benfleet – The word Benfleet derives from the Saxon word 'Beamfleote' which means 'an inlet of creek within woods close by'

Little Burstead sign

Ramsden Bellhouse

Wickford – Combining the Saxon word 'Wic' to mean either 'dairy farm' or 'castle' with 'ford' meaning 'a shallow place in a body of water, such as a river'

The symbol was created in 1951, but was not adopted by the Basildon District Council as the official badge until 1992.

It is divided into four, with each quadrant displaying a different area of the District. In the centre is a redesigned image of the 'Mother & Child' statue which represents the New Town.

Top Left: **The Mayflower** – remembering the pilgrim to America by some of Billericay's residents in 1620.

Top Right: **The Corn Sheaf and Scythe** – showing the important farming heritage of Wickford.

Bottom Right: **The Mallard rising from the Marshland** – a reference to the wetlands of Pitsea.

Bottom Left: **The Church on the Hill** – An image of St Nicholas Church in Laindon.

Churches of Basildon

All Saints, Vange

The oldest church in the area, the structure of All Saints dates back to the 12th century. You can find it hidden away behind a row of bushes, opposite where the Basildon Zoo once stood on London Road. No longer used as a place of worship, All Saints was declared redundant in 1996. However in 2003, the Churches Conservation Trust took over the task of restoring and preserving the church back to its former glory. The building itself may no longer be in use, but the graves in the church yard are still regularly visited, cared for and maintained.

St Michael's Church, Pitsea

The remains of St Michael's church can be found on top of the Pitsea Mount, over looking the 24hour Tesco's. All that's left today is the tower, alter and a concrete outline of the former church. The tower was last rebuilt in 1870 and since then the main structure has been taken down for safety reasons and replaced by a 'compass viewing guide' and some benches. The demise of the church started in the 70's and after several failed attempts to salvage, it was eventually taken on by the

All Saints Church, Vange

communications company, Orange, who now use the tower as a mobile phone base station (a mast).

To the West of the church tower lies the burial place of the Freeman family. On the epitaph of daughter, Ann Freeman, the bizarre inscription reads "Here lies a weak and sinful worm, the vilest of her race, Saved through gods electing love, his free and sovereign grace". Very little is known as to why such damning words were chosen to record the death of this woman. What is known of Ann Freeman is that she was born in March 1837 and spent most of her life as a domestic servant, before dying of heart disease in 1879, aged 42. There are rumours that suggest Ann was possibly accused of being a witch, although there is little evidence to confirm this theory.

St Michael's Church

St Peter's Church, Nevendon

This 13th Century church is nestled snugly in between the houses of Nevendon. It is very well looked after by the congregation and is the hub of many social activities organised in the parish.

St Martins Church, Town Centre, Basildon

The Bishop of Chelmsford, Rt. Rev. John Tiarks, conducted the first service on 10th November 1962, officially opening the church to the public. Eleven years later, on November 3rd 1973 the garden of remembrance was opened and then in 1989 the plain glass windows were replaced by an impressive stained glass design created by Joseph Nuttgens.

To celebrate the 50th anniversary of the town and opening of the newly built glass Bell tower, a special service was held in the church with VIP guests of honour, Queen Elizabeth II and her husband the Duke of Edinburgh.

St Nicholas Church, Laindon

The most renowned church in the area, it even features on the Basildon District Symbol as a representation of Laindon.

The church was built in the 13th Century with the west end timber annexe (the priest house) being added sometime in the 17th Century. In the mid 1990's the church was given the status of a Grade I listed building.

In 1837 the priest house became home to the first school in the area, named Puckles School, after local landowner John Puckle, who donated all of his land to the church after his death in 1617.

A sermon is held every year, on St John's Day, in remembrance of Mr Puckle. There is also a charity set up in his honour which was responsible for paying the salary of the school masters. The attic of the priest house was used to accommodate six local farmers' boys who attended the school as boarders. The room was far from luxurious with just one very small glass tile in place of a window.

The last school master to teach there was James Hornsby, who was born in 1804 with the lower part of his left arm missing. Before becoming a school master he was a horseman on a local farm, a parish clerk and also a sexton (grave digger). It was said that Mr Hornsby was a strict disciplinarian, and was reported that he had, on occasion, tied the children who had misbehaved to the belfry beams as form of punishment.

Hornsby lived in the damp and draughty Priest House, and it is these poor living conditions which were credited as being the possible reason for the deaths of his three wives. His first wife Sarah died in August 1851, his second Catherine in February 1859 and his third and final wife, also named Catherine, died in March 1883. James Hornsby himself lived to the ripe old age of 83, finally coming to rest in May 1887. His grave and those of his three wives can be found to the west of the church, beside the Priest House.

It is believed that the belfry beams of the church, were in fact taken from ships active in the Spanish Armada, this however is not confirmed, and it is possible that the rumour started simply by the fact that the church's tenor bell dates from 1588, the same year of the Armada.

Holy Cross, Basildon

Holy Cross Chapel was first recorded in 1230 as part of the Manor of Botelers, which later became Moat House Farm. A piece of the moat which once surrounded the manor is now being used as a private fishing lake, to which you can access by a path running along side the Fryerns Social Club (The Hole in the Wall).

The nave of the church dates from the 14th century and the majority of the rest from the 15th century, with the church being fully restored in 1701.

Holy Cross Church, Basildon

There are several reports by locals claiming to have seen a ghostly figure, wearing a red robe, in the court yard of the church. The "Crimson Monk" made national headlines in 1964 when television crews, photographers and newspaper journalists came to stage a stake out. Claims were made over a period of months by 10 different cleaners, on route to and from work, at the Ford's tractor plant. This triggered media frenzy. Unsurprisingly the ghost 'chose' not to appear on the night when the whole area had been brightly illuminated by the TV crews industrial size lighting equipment.

There are some 'loose' facts which support the ghost sighing claims. Firstly there have been two previous priests of the church which had been monks, James Daven (1483) and John Hogeskynne (1544). There had also been a previous rector of Basildon who later became a Dean of a London Church, a position which would have required him to wear a crimson gown.

St Margaret's, Bowers Gifford

The church was built in the 14th century by Sir John Gifford, with an incomplete brass of the Lord of the Manor, remaining to this day, inside the church.

The bell tower contains 3 bells, said to be amongst the oldest in the county.

There is also a large raised plot, defined by a stone wall, where local landowner and business man, Harold Howard, is lay to rest alongside several members of his family.

Harold Howard's Vision for Pitsea

Harold George Howard was a local landowner and business man. 'Howard Dairies' had eight distribution depots and 30 shops including premises at Pitsea, Laindon, Southernhay, Whitmore Way and Timberlog Lane. The dairy employed a total of 1,000 people and was responsible for supplying 75,000 customers with it products.

Mr Howard, who once lived at Bluehouse Farm, was fascinated by Tudor architecture and went about designing a Tudor style town at Pitsea. The first building to be built was 'The Railway Hotel' later to become known simply as 'The Railway'. The pub was closed in 2006 and has remained unoccupied ever since.

Harold Howard then went on to create more Tudor buildings - Pitsea Broadway (originally a cinema but now a bingo hall), Tudor Mansions and Tudor Chambers (which now include a kebab shop, a video store, a taxi rank and a estate agent), and Anne Boleyn Mansions (the Lloyds TSB building).

A residential street and park has since been renamed in his honour. Howard Crescent with its mock Tudor design is situated next to, what was once called Beckney Mead, and is now known as Howard Park.

After the war and the invention of the New Town, Howard was forced to give up on his idea of creating a 'Tudor Town' at Pitsea and was ordered to hand over his land to the Billericay Council. A speech was

Anne Boleyn Mansions

Howard Crescent

Tudor Chambers

made by Howard declaring his disappointment at not being able to continue with his vision. *"Neither I nor my son will be able to complete my dream. It is like an unfinished symphony"*

To commemorate those who lost their lives between the two World Wars, Harold Howard privately funded a war memorial which once stood outside the Railway pub and can now be found in Harold Park.

In 1961, three months after celebrating his Golden Wedding Anniversary with wife Rose, Harold George Howard passed away at his home and was buried at the family plot, within the grounds of St Margaret's Church, Bowers Gifford.

Royal Visits

'Love them or hate them' a public appearance by a member of the Royal family is always going to draw in the crowds and make the next days headlines.

Basildon has received many Royal visits over the years, with the first taking place on Saturday 8th September 1956, when Princess Alice, Countess of Athlone opened the Langdon Hills Methodist Church.

The most famous visit took place on the 12th March 1999. Queen Elizabeth II accompanied by her husband, the Duke of Edinburgh unveiled a commemorative plague inside the Basildon Centre to mark the 50th anniversary of the New Town. Her Majesty and the Duke also officially opened the glass Bell Tower, in the town centre and attended a special service at St Martin's church.

This was the Queens first visit to Basildon, her husband Phillip had been here once before, nearly 40 years previous. On 4th March 1960 a red helicopter, piloted by the Prince, landed in a field near Christopher Martin Road. His visit was to the Carrera's Cigarette Factory where he made history by 'throwing a switch' to start the first totally automatic cigarette making machine in the world!

The Duke and Duchess of Gloucester made a visit to the town on

26th June 1957. The couple opened the new major road, Southernhay, and also paid personal visits to the homes of many of the town's residents. In addition to this, they made an appearance at the official naming of the park and recreational area which was being built on the edge of the town centre - Gloucester Park.

In 1964, on 3rd November the Queen Mother made a visit to open the new homes at Southwood Court (Printer's Pension Corporation) in Great Spenders. The popular Royal made a speech and unveiled a plaque, before taking off in another red helicopter from Holy Cross recreation ground. Unlike the Duke of Edinburgh, the Queen Mother did not occupy the role as helicopter pilot, choosing to travel instead as a passenger.

Prince Edward, the youngest child of Queen Elizabeth II, opened the Eastgate Centre, which at the time, back in 1985, was the largest shopping centre in Essex.

On 26th of September 1990 the newly built St Luke's Hospice was officially opened by the Duchess of Norfolk. Later that year, in November, The hospice was to receive yet another Royal visit in the form of Diana, Princess of Wales.

Princess Anne's visit to Basildon Hospital on 11th April 2003 resulted in her naming the newest ward block - the Jubilee Block, in honour of the recent celebration for the Queens 50 years as head of state.

Community

Within the district of Basildon, there are plenty of opportunities for those wanting to participate in activities of a sporting, artistic or social nature. Details of such clubs, groups and societies can be found at the library, the internet or in the local newspapers. With such a wide variety available there should be something out there to suit everybody.

I personally visited a number of Basildon's local groups, many of which are included in this section of the book. Throughout my visits I found the organisers and members to be very friendly, accommodating and interesting people.

I witnessed a strong closeness and belonging by all the participants, as well as a real sense of community spirit.

Also included in this section of the book - How the community of Basildon is connected, through the twinning programme, to towns in France and Germany. I personally visited each of the towns to learn about the community, culture and lives of its residents.

Basildon United Football Club

Basildon United FC, nicknamed The Bee's after their distinctive 'black and gold' home strip, was formed in 1967 and started out in the Thurrock Thames-side Combination League, where they competed for just one season before joining the Greater London League.

They were granted senior status by the Essex County FA in 1970 and the club became one of the founder members of the Essex Senior League. After four consecutive championships, Basildon United applied for, and was granted, promotion into the Athenian League in 1980. The following season they gained promoted again taking them up into the Isthmian League, Division Two. It took just three years before Basildon United topped the league as Champions in 1984 earning them promotion once more into the Isthmian League, Division One.

The climb through the leagues came to an end in 1989 when Basildon United suffered relegation for the first time in the clubs history. After a couple of years back in Division Two, the Isthmian League was 'de-regionalised'. As a result of having to travel such long distances for away games, the club struggled financially and they were forced to rejoin the Essex Senior League for the start of the 1991/92 season.

In the 1993/4 season Basildon United won the Essex Senior League 'double', making them league record holders, having won the competition a total of 5 times.

Basildon United club crest

Basildon United continue to compete in the Essex Senior League which is at level 9 in the English Football League System (or Football Pyramid). This means that Basildon United FC is 'hypothetically' less than 10 seasons away from promotion to the Barclays Premier League.

The team play their home games at the Zone International Stadium, nicknamed 'The Hive', in Gardiners Close, Basildon. For many years there has been talk of development in the area which leaves the clubs future at this site uncertain.

The first game to be played at the Gardiners Close ground was a friendly against a West Ham XI on 11th August 1970. Amongst the 3600 spectators were, ex England and West Ham stars, Geoff Hurst and Jimmy Greaves.

In October 1979, the club had floodlights installed at a cost of £10,000. A friendly was arranged to commemorate the purchase, with Crystal Palace as opposition, and approximately 2000 spectators in attendance on the evening.

Basildon United playing at 'The Hive'

Famous Ex-Players of Basildon United

Steve Tilson – Current manager and ex-player of Southend United

Jonathon Gould – Goalkeeper who played 110 times for Celtic and twice for Scotland.

Kerry Dixon – Ex Chelsea and England striker played briefly for Basildon United in 97/98.

David Cusack – Played for Sheffield Wednesday, Southend United & Millwall and is currently a director at Basildon United.

Michael Kightly – Goal scoring midfielder at Wolverhampton Wanderers and has a number of England U21 caps.

Player Profiles

Name: Richard Mann
Position: Goalkeeper

Richard is playing his first season with the Bees having previously played for Arsenal, Leyton orient, Southend, Hullbridge and East Thurrock.

He was a part of the Hullbridge under 18s team which won the Essex Country Cup Final in Billericay, and also played for Arsenal at the U15 level.

Name: Scott Fairbrass
Position: Centre Forward

Scott has so far played just the one season for Basildon United. Previously clubs include Ilford first XI, Concord, Basildon Town, Southend United YTS and East Anglia Boys.

He recalls his playing highlight as winning the Dana Cup in Denmark, where he represented England at the age of 14, reaching the final and beating the Germans before a crowd of 12,000 spectators.

Name: Dan 'Butts' Butler
Position: Right Back

Dan has been at Basildon United for 4 months, previously playing Sunday League football in Dagenham and at Hertfordshire Uni. He loves seeing Basildon United's results appear in a national newspaper every Sunday and excitedly recalls how on one particular week Basildon Utd were listed next to Real Madrid.

Basildon & Pitsea Cricket Club

The cricket club's origins pre-date the Second World War. During the conflicts they temporary disbanded, reforming some years later in 1948.

The Basildon Cricket Club played their games at the Old Rectory in Cranes Farm Road, which is now the site of the New Holland Tractor Plant.

Whilst the New Town was being built the club relocated to Benfleet, returning in 1962 when they merged with Basildon Cranes and moved to their current Mopsies Park address. The clubhouse and practice nets were bought by the club with the pitches leased from the council, thus saving on maintenance costs. The club house, which was officially opened in 1982 by Essex C.C. players - Stuart Turner and Brian Hardie, is equipped with changing facilities, showers and a bar 'Charlies Arms' which was named in memory of lifelong member of the club Charlie Reeves (1919-2001)

In 1997 Basildon C.C. merged with the Pitsea C.C. to form The Basildon & Pitsea Cricket Club. They currently run 5 weekend teams, plus regular weekday games as well as several youth projects. There is a very close and friendly atmosphere at the club with an active social side off the pitch for all its members.

The 2007/08 season saw the 1st XI cling on to survival in Division

Basildon and Pitsea Cricket Club badge

Basildon and Pitsea Cricket Club

One, with the very last game of the season deciding their fate. They narrowly avoided the drop back down to Division Two, from which they were promoted the previous year.

Club President and founding member, Bob Ayres, has been with the club for over 50 years, having only retired from playing two seasons ago. Bob made his first maiden century aged 37 and took an impressive "9 wickets for 17 runs" aged 71 years old.

Throughout his time at the club Bob has won the 'Basildon Knock Out Cup' a total of 7 times, and was captain of the side which won the 'Southend Knock Out Cup' in 1974. He has also captained the Essex Cricket Association side.

In 2007 Bob received a 'Long Service Award' from the Essex County Cricket Board and was subsequently nominated for an OSCA (Outstanding Service to Cricket Award) by the ECA (English Cricket Association).

"This is a very progressive club, involving all aspects of cricket from ages 8 years and upwards" Bob Ayres 2008

Player Profiles

Name: Frank McLeod
Position: Batsman

Originally from Sydney, Australia, Frank has played with the club for 7 years, describing himself as "a middle order batsman, occasional bowler and mentor to the younger players". He is also the only current Basildon & Pitsea player to have scored an Essex League First XI century. His previous clubs before joining Basildon & Pitsea span across 3 continents: King George V (Hong Kong), Vagabonds (HK), St Georges (HK) Kowloon Cricket Club Templar's (HK), Waverley District CC (Sydney, Australia), Rockdale RSL (AUS), Illawong CC (AUS), Eastern Suburbs (AUS) Eastbourne CC (UK), Sidley CC (UK) and Polegate CC (UK)

"I have enjoyed my time at the club due to the friendliness and camaraderie throughout all the teams"

Name: Brian Waterman
Position: Batsman and Lifelong member of the club

I.T. manager, Brian has been a member of the club for 40 years, before which he played with the Basildon Cranes, who in 1968 amalgamated with Basildon C.C.

Brian remembers fondly making 44 runs for the team which won the 'Southend Knock-out Competition' in 1974. Throughout his time at the club, Brian has racked up 5 centuries, including one recently in the 2007/08 season.

"Basildon and Pitsea C.C. has been a way of life to me for 40 years now, with the club having its ups and downs over the years. Currently it is doing very well and there is a great atmosphere at the club. It's like being part of a large family."

Name: Wayne Morgan
Position: Opening Bowler

Wayne, originally from Barbados in the West Indies, has been with the club for 36 years now, having previously played with Langdon Hills C.C, Westleigh C.C. and Fords XI C.C. The highlight of Wayne's playing career would have to be the time he took 7 wickets (for 26 runs off 26 overs) against Hornchurch C.C. Wayne's role at the club extends beyond his efforts on the cricket field as he is also the club house manager.

"Over the years I worked my way from the 3rd XI up to the 1st XI and I am now working my way back down!"

C&K Basildon Ladies FC

Basildon Town FC is the oldest football club in the Basildon, having been formed in 1946. C&K Basildon Ladies FC (formerly Basildon Town Ladies FC) became a part of this set up in 2004, after splitting from nearby rivals Basildon United FC.

The club is based at the Selex Sports & Leisure Club (old Marconi Club), where they have access to two full size pitches, changing facilities, club bar and function room.

Peter King, Team Manager / Hon Secretary of the club, is a Level 1 FA Coach and actively encourages all of his players, aged 16 and above, to also take their Level 1 badges. This allows them to better appreciate the correct coaching techniques and assist in training the clubs younger members. C&K Basildon currently have 7 players qualified to FA Level 1, with one player having achieved her Level 2 badge.

The club currently runs three affiliated league sides, 2 ladies (over 16 years of age) plus an under 15's side. They also have a group of U11's who will play 'friendlies' for the first season.

In the 2007/08 season, the Ladies team gained promotion to the Essex Women's League Division 1, after what turned out to be a thoroughly thrilling campaign.

C&K Basildon Ladies FC

C&K Basildon Ladies FC

Peter King describes how this became such an important chapter in the history of C&K Basildon Ladies FC:

"In early April, we sat in 3rd place on equal points with the 2nd place team, our goal-difference was inferior to theirs but we still had a game to play. That game was against the already confirmed Champions 'Hannakins' who up until that point had won all 15 of the season's league games"

"The game was scheduled for the 4th May 2008 and all we needed was a point to secure 2nd place and automatic promotion. We decided to react to the challenge as a professional team would and agreed to consultation with my Son (who has recently graduated in Sports Psychology) He advised us that we needed 'carbs' 24 hours before the game and lean cuisine (proteins) the morning of the game. So we had a pasta party at my house on the Saturday evening with plenty of team bonding (computer games, monopoly, trivial pursuits etc) followed with a lean cuisine breakfast on Sunday morning again at my house."

"On the day of the game, two of my senior players presented me with a match ball, A Champions League Adidas football which they had taken to church that morning and got the vicar to bless for us!"

"Well the game plan worked. We totally frustrated Hannakins and apart from a couple of near misses we secured the 0-0 result which was what we needed."

"12 bottles of cheap champagne were shared amongst the two teams so that the compulsory spraying could take place; I had just become the Manager of a promoted team!"

"An hour after the game I was called out onto the pitch where I was presented with the 'Blessed ball' with every panel suitably inscribed and signed by all the first team players and given to me as a memento.

"It now has pride of place in my trophy cabinet! I have never been so happy about a sporting triumph as I was that weekend. To work with these wonderful Ladies and to win promotion was my sporting highlight."

Player Profiles

Name: Louise Pike
Playing Position: Centre Back / Defence

Louise, a teacher at Chafford Hundred Campus Secondary School, has been with the club since it started back in 2004, having previously played for Stifford Clays Ladies FC. Southend United supporter, Louise, recalls last seasons 0-0 draw with Hannakins Ladies and achieving promotion to be her all time playing highlight.

Name: Eike Mangold
Playing Position: Midfield / Striker

Eike, the C&K international star, has been with the club since the very beginning but took a break from the team to work as a programmer for the UN in Afghanistan. She returned in time to be part of the promotion winning side last season. Speaking about the final game against Hannakins she said "It was the biggest match I have ever played in, everyone was outstanding!" In her home country of Germany, Eike played ladies football for TUS Rotenhof, BTSV, RTSV & HSV. She now lives in Laindon, works as a web developer for Sony and is also responsible for maintaining the C&K Basildon Ladies website.

Name: Kira Lewis
Playing Position: Goalkeeper

Kira is studying Sports and Exercise Science at Seevic College where she has been part of the college football team for 3 seasons. In 2006/07 she was named player of the year and in July 2007 joined C&K Basildon Ladies. In January 2008 she was spotted by coaches at Crystal Palace and has since signed with the London club and played in the Surrey Cup final against Chelsea.

Name: Aishatu Shuaibu
Playing Position: Striker

Aishatu, the clubs star striker, has averaged nearly a goal a game in the past two years. A keen supporter of Arsenal & Arsenal Ladies, Aishatu will unfortunately not play such a prominent part in the upcoming seasons as she will be off at University studying Forensic Science.

Basildon Disabled Sports and Social Club

The Basildon Disabled Club was formed in 1981 by a gentleman named Mervin Potter, who sadly passed away approximately 10 years ago. Local taxi company 'DAVITA' helped Mervin fund the club, which for the first 17 years held weekly meetings at the Pitsea Leisure Centre. The current location of the club at the Swan Mead Centre on Church Road, became available in 1996 with the club moving in the following year.

The club is now run by husband and wife duo Colin and Betty Jeffrey. Betty, a wheelchair user herself, has represented Great Britain in both shooting and table tennis. She is also a former ladies arm wrestling champion and has held National records for both Javelin and Shot Put.

The Basildon Disabled Club caters for people with various disabilities, providing a fun and relaxed social environment for all its members. In addition to this there are many activities available including shooting, archery, short mat bowls, table tennis and pool. During the summer months the club holds their annual Sports Day of 20 events including track and field.

The club competes alongside able-bodied teams in the Basildon &

Betty Jeffrey

District Table Tennis League – Division 3 and this season there have been some good individual performances from its members.

Meetings are held three times a week - Tuesday and Fridays, between 10am and 230pm and Monday evenings, between 7pm and 9pm. Membership fees for adults are £20.00 a year plus £2.00 a week subs and for children £10.00 per annum, £1.50 per week subs.

Basildon Disabled Club member, Adam Fontain, was just 7 years old when he suffered 2 strokes leaving him paralysed down the left hand side of his body. Doctors at the time warned his parents that he may never walk again. Eleven years later and Adam is not only walking, but winning medals at both National and International level for Air Rifle Shooting. Adam now trains with the Disability Shooting Great British Team and looks set to compete in the 2012 Paralympics. His talent has already seen him compete in Luxemburg, Slovakia and Turkey with an exciting opportunity for Adam to take part in the 2009 Oceania Games held in Sydney, Australia.

Adam, along with his mother Christine, who helps out at the club, were invited to be guests on the ITV Good Morning Show where they

Table tennis - one of the many activities available at the club

were asked to tell their story on National Television to presenters Phillip Schofield and Fern Brittan.

In addition to money collected by way of membership fees and subs, the Basildon Disabled Club relies heavily on the generosity of the people and businesses of Basildon to allow them to continue their great work.

Collection boxes can be found all around the town, with one at 'Ocean Blue', the recently re-opened fish restaurant at East Walk in the Town Centre. Six years ago whilst representatives of the club were out fundraising, restaurant owner Aziz Hassan saw their efforts and gave them all free lunches, he also offered to put a collection box on the counter in his shop. In November 2007 a fire meant the restaurant was to close for nearly 10 months whilst refurbishments took place. Aziz however managed to salvage the box, including its contents, and has to date raised an impressive £210 for the club.

If your interested in joining the club, or making a donation, you can contact Betty or Colin at 01268 473973 or 01268 530577.

"The aims of the organisation are to build confidence through social activities and achievement in sport."

Member Profiles

Name: Peter M

Peter who suffers from epilepsy has been coming to the club for over 4 years and attends twice weekly. During a rather nasty fit, he hit his head and severely fractured his skull leaving him almost totally deaf.

He describes the social aspect as being his favourite thing about the club, as well as playing pool. Peter is a keen Arsenal fan and has a season ticket for the Premier League club.

Name: Andrew W

In 1990 Andrew was working as a scaffolder when he fell from a faulty tower, resulting in a lengthy period of intensive care with ½ of his skull having collapsed. Originally from Pitsea, but now living in Billericay, Andrew has been coming to the club for nearly 10 years. Andrew enjoys meeting people and his favourite activities are short mat bowls and pool.

Name: Adam F

At the age of 7, Adam suffered two strokes and became paralysed down his left side. 11 years later he is part of the Great British shooting team and is looking to compete in the 2012 Paralympics. Adam attends the club as often as possible which gives him the opportunity to train. Adam is also a member of the Table Tennis team which competes in the Basildon League.

Vange & Pitsea Amateur Boxing Club

The Vange & Pitsea ABC was started in January 2005. The founding members, led by Frank Doyle, felt that the area was lacking somewhere that kids could improve their fitness, learn a sport, make friends and be taught discipline & respect.

The council owned Glenmere Centre, became available and the club set up there on Tuesday, Wednesday and Thursday evenings. They are hoping to move into their own property soon and have been looking at the possibility of taking over the land attached to the back of V&P Working Mans Club, for which they are currently awaiting planning permission.

There are approximately 80 members of the club (with 50 who attend regularly). The cost of membership is just £3.00 a session, payable on a pay-as-you-go basis. The ages range from 7 years old to adult with several members competing nationwide. Once the club feels a person is ready, both physically and mentally, they encourage the members to apply to be 'carded', which allows them to fight against other clubs.

Training is based on a rotation system, controlled by a bell, which tells the boxers when it is time to move onto the next station. Activities include shadow boxing (in front of mirrors), punch bags & skipping. There is full supervision and assistance offered by the many qualified coaches and helpers. The club has a sparring ring which they have set up on training nights. They also have a full size professional ring, but unfortunately there is not the space at the present location to be able to use it.

All equipment, including safety gear, is supplied by the club. Members will receive personal attention from the trainers, with individual one-on-one tuitions throughout the sessions to help members focus on their specific needs and monitor their level of progress.

Funds are raised by the organisers, and in addition to money made from membership fees, the club creates extra income through raffles in the Vange & Pitsea WMC. In 2007 they received a donation from the Amateur Boxing Association (ABA) Boxing Foundation Fund, of £200 worth of equipment.

The club holds an annual "presentation night" where the members are awarded trophies and medals to commemorate their progress and successes throughout the year. Well known faces in the boxing world, such as Jason Rowland (light welterweight from West Ham who in 2001 fought Ricky Hatton.) and Basildon's very own undisputed World Champion -Terry Marsh - have in the past given their time to congratulate members and distribute the awards.

Player Profiles

Name: Michael Murnane
Age / Weight: 22 years old / 60kgs

Michael is a window fitter from Basildon who has been boxing for nearly 10 years. He has been with the club since it started back in 2005 having previously been part of Chalvedon ABC.

He has so far competed in 43 matches (winning 34). List of honours include: The school boy championships, NABC Championships, Essex Championships and a Bronze medal for England in the Four Nations Amateur Boxing Championships.

Frank in the ring with sparring members

Vange and Pitsea Amateur Boxing Club

Name: Connor Mulvey
Age / Weight: 21 years old / 60kgs

Connor is a plasterer from Basildon who started competing in 2009, having won 3 out of 3 fights to date.

He originally got involved with the club for fitness reasons, having noted that he was going out and drinking too much, he wanted to get himself back into shape and boxing seemed an appealing way of doing that.

Name: Grant Tony Lee Richards
Age / Weight: 19 years old / 64kgs

Originally from Barking, Grant recently moved to the area and joined the club to keep up his fitness levels and improve on his ability.

He enjoys the training sessions, especially sparring, and gets along well with the trainers and other boxers at the club.

Essex Spartans

The Essex Spartans were an amalgamation of two old Football rivals - the Essex Chiefs and Redbridge Fire (Champions of Brit Bowl XI in 1997). The Spartans were formed in January 1999 and have since been looked after financially by St Lawrence Holiday Home Park. Additional sponsorship this season came from - 'Sorrells Wine Racks' & 'Tube Lines'.

The Essex Chiefs were founded by Tony Palmer in 1985, and Tony is still today at the helm of the Essex Spartans setup as General Manager of the club.

The Spartans originally played their home games in Wanstead (London Borough of Redbridge, East London). After a short time, they moved to Eaton Manor Rugby Club and then onto the Astroturf in Gloucester Park. After a few years at the Basildon location, the Council announced that they were no longer allowed to use it, as money from the FA (Football Association) was going to be used to resurface it. They were moved to Hannakins Farm, Billericay in 2005 and have been there ever since.

In 2008, the Essex Spartans became twinned with Billerica Memorial High School in Billerica, Massachusetts as a part of the town of Billericay's Town twinning programme.

The Spartans play their football in the BAFL2 (British American Football League 2) which consists of a total of 27 teams. – The league is broken up into five regional divisions. The Essex Spartans compete in the South East Conference with long standing rivals the Maidstone Puma's, the Colchester Gladiators, London Cobras and the East Kent Mavericks.

There is also a selection of Essex Spartans merchandise available, including match shirts, baseball caps, polo shirts, t-shirts, sweatshirts, hoodies, shorts, rain jackets and car mini shirt (with sucker) all emblazoned with the teams' logo and designs.

The Essex Spartans are always looking to recruit new players at both senior and junior levels, and would love to see some more fans coming along and supporting their local British American Football team.

Essex Spartans

A message from the Club Founder and Team Manager – Tony Palmer.

"Why not come over to Hannikans Farm, Billericay and try a new sport. One couple came along to watch a game over 15 years ago and have been supporting the team regularly ever since, they seem to like it, and so might you"

If you are interested in finding out more, take a look at the website at www.essexspartans.co.uk

Player Profiles

Name: Craig Brittney
Playing Position: Outside Lineback / Free Safety / Defensive Back Coach

Craig has been with the Spartans since 1993, back when the club was still based in Basildon. Craig missed a couple of seasons though injury but has since returned to playing. He played previously for Southend Sabres Youth where they were crowned National Champions in 1992. Craig played in the Great Britain Crusaders 1992 team Vs USA All-stars and in 1997 was named the Essex Spartans defensive player of the year.

"The Spartans have produced some great players over the years and have had some bitter Essex rivalries during that time"

Name: Ashley Christopher Faiers
Playing Position: Cornerback & Safety

In 2008 Ashley stepped up to Senior League having played 2.5 years at youth level. He started playing British American Football after the football (soccer) team he played for folded.

"In what other sport can you hurt someone and get away with it?"

Name: Scott Smallman
Playing Position: WR, TE, Kick Off & Kick Return

Scott has so far played just one season with the Spartans. A student at the University of Teesside in Middlesbrough, he also plays for a team in the North East called the Teeside Cougers. His highlight so far has been playing in the Northern Division Play Offs and he hopes for many more to come.

"In my first ever play I became lead blocking for the Running Back scoring a 55 yard Touch Down"

Basildon Players

The local Amateur Dramatics society has been entertaining the people of Basildon with their plays, musicals and pantomimes for over 45 years.

In 1963, a gentleman named Duncan McKeggie officially formed the 'Basildon Players'. Their first performance, a comedy play 'The Long Christmas Dinner' was scheduled for the following year. The Basildon Players have since produced more than 130 shows, averaging around 3 a year. In 2008 they performed 'Aladdin', 'Sweeny Todd' and 'Agatha Christie's - A Murder is Announced' all of which were showcased at the Mirren Studio in the Towngate Theatre.

In addition to their major shows a 'War Time Revue' was presented at the Langdon Hills Methodist Church in September called 'Memories of Bert & Ada'. The hour long spectacle was performed by a cast made up mostly by the groups least experienced members. The audience were treated to a humorous and nostalgic look back at the musical acts which have topped the charts over the years including Shirley Temple, Al Johnson, The Beatles, Spandau Ballet and ending with a modern hip hop medley.

The most recent Basildon Players offering 'Agatha Christies - A Murder is Announced' was directed by veteran member Trevor Bavin, with three consecutive evening shows, and a Saturday matinee staged over

Basildon Players

a weekend in October 2008. The amateur cast gave impressive professional performances and were greatly received by the audience.

The 'players' meet every Monday and Wednesday at Woodlands School in Kingswood. There is a relaxed atmosphere, where fun and laughter is mixed in with the serious business of learning lines and rehearsing scenes.

A former member of the Basildon Players, Nathan Guy, has since gone on to appear in many professional plays and pantomimes throughout the country. He is now a cast member of the award winning stage show – Lazy Town Live – an adaptation of the popular children's TV programme. Nathan plays the part of Stingy, a materialistic 6 year old who dreams of one day becoming King.

"I remember Nathan when he first came to us at school age, it's a real buzz to see him on stage – I'm so proud of him" Karen Barton (a member of the Basildon Players for over 18 years)

'Memories of Bert and Ada'
A war time revue

Player Profiles

Merlyn Buckley

One of the more recent additions to the Basildon Players team, Merlyn joined with no previous experience making his first amateur dramatics performance in the 2008 Sweeny Todd production. *"I didn't play any major part [court usher], but it was major enough for me at the time, it was totally new to me, great fun and one of the best things I have ever done. I really like acting although I have not done much of it. I don't even know if I am any good at it yet"*

"Basildon Players are a great bunch of people, all unique, good folk. By joining I have gained some brilliant friends. I feel that it is good to have an artistic outlet, it's still early days but this is something I find really fun and always challenging".

Joyce Farrow

As Basildon Players longest serving member, Joyce has been with the amateur dramatics group for over 30 years. She is also club treasurer and was once a secretary to a professional acting family.

Joyce first hit the stage in a Basildon Players production called "No Time for Fig Leaves" and recollects being quite nervous, fearing that she would not be able to 'pull it off'

Her favourite of all the Basildon Players shows, called 'Dark of the Moon' was performed at the old Towngate Theatre in the 1980's. She played the part of the Black Witch and described it as being a "wonderful play and wonderful production"

"I rarely act these days but enjoy watching the others perform, although I can be very critical. I also like to help out the newcomers when ever possible"

Trevor Bavin

The first main role Trevor played was as Dame "Sadie Spangle" in a pantomime of Goldilocks. Like many of the other members Trevor joined having no previous acting experience and now having been with the

Basildon Players for over 15 years Trevor now not only performs but has directed many of the shows including, most recently, the Agatha Christie murder mystery.

"I have found my time with the Basildon Players to be amazing. We have a great circle of friends and the whole experience has been magical"

John Spriggs

One of the more experienced members of the group, John gained previous experience with the Basildon Operatic Society, Church nativities and the Southend Operatic Society before joining the Basildon Players nearly 18 years ago.

John's introduction to acting came during Missionary work at a church evening in which he played a small Nigerian boy. The part required him to say three words in Yoruba (a regional language of Africa).

"The best thing about being a player is the interaction with other people, seeing them in many different roles and watching how they develop over the years."

Basildon Philatelic Society
Philately - the collection and study of postage stamps

The collection of stamps is said to be the "World's Most Popular Hobby" with tens of millions of people worldwide actively involved.

Collections can be personalised to suit particular interests. Some collections will be limited to particular countries, or more precisely to a specific time period during the history of that country. Others will choose 'Thematic' or 'Topical' collections, where instead of its geography, a collection is based on the image displayed on the stamp i.e. cars, birds, sports, celebrities... The possibilities are endless.

The Basildon Philatelic Society was formed by employees of the Basildon Urban District Council, during a meeting held at Woodlands Boys School in July 1968. The venue of the meetings has since changed several times before settling in 2000 at the George Hurd Centre, Cherrydown West. In 2008 the centre was demolished and rebuilt at a site on Audley Way (off Broadmayne), where the club now holds their twice monthly meetings.

The Society includes the following activities at their meetings and special functions – auctions, competitions, dinners, exchange packets, film shows, informal evenings, quizzes, guest speakers, stamp days & fairs, as well as visits to other societies and places of interest.

The evening upon which I attended, the group were holding a 'recent

40 year anniversary BPS presentation pack

acquisitions' meeting. Members were given the opportunity to display parts of their collections, accompanied by a short presentation. There were approximately 20 members in attendance and the atmosphere was happy, friendly and relaxed.

One member specialised in colleting stamps specifically from Australia, New Zealand, Fiji, Jamaica and Barbados. He told the group how he had bought additions for his New Zealand collection, for which he paid just a few pounds. Amongst the set he found one particular stamp, which on its own had a value of over £400. Proving that not only is it an interesting and enjoyable pastime but can also be a profitable one as well.

Another Basildon Philatelic Society member, Mr JF Cowlin, gave a presentation on part of his collection to the group. He collects war themed pieces, in particular the Boer War and French Revolution. On display were notes, letters and transcripts which have survived from each of these conflicts. Philately does not necessarily focus solely on the stamps itself, but anything which could be considered 'stamp related'. In this case it was something which had, in one form or another, been passed though the postal system.

Basildon Philatelic Society

Len Stanway, (President, Treasurer & Packet Secretary for the Society) gave a presentation on '2008 Singapore' which documented the first 8 months of the year within the country. Included were a series of stamps celebrating the first ever race in Formula 1 history to be held at night through the streets of Singapore.

In 2008 The Basildon Philatelic Society celebrated its 40th anniversary by hosting Stamp Essex 2008 which was held at James Hornsby School, Laindon. In addition to this they issued their very own commemorative 40th Anniversary Stamp designed by Society Chairman, Charlie Meads.

For more information you can visit their website www.basildon.aeps.org.uk

Member Profiles

Name: David Church
Status: A stamp dealer from Laindon

It was David's father who first introduced him to stamp collecting. He is now a full time Stamp Dealer and has been a member of the Basildon Philatelic Society for some 40 years. The one thing David enjoys most about the BPS is how he gets to see a variety of different collections as well as the social aspect of being part of a club. This is not the first time David has featured in a book about Basildon. Peter Lucas' 'Basildon - Birth of a City' (published in 1986) includes a photograph of a very young David receiving a haircut from local barber Bill Barrett. David's mother remembers the day the photograph was taken but had no idea the picture would later appear in a book.

Name: Charlie Meads
Status: Retired Civil Servant from Basildon.

Charlie was just 6 years old when he started collecting stamps, his father would bring stamps, from all over the world, home from his work at a cigarette manufacturers. Charlie is the Chairman of the Basildon Philatelic Society and the editor of its newsletter 'The Basildon Stamp Collector'. He is also responsible for the creation and upkeep of the clubs website.

Name: Geoff Miller
Status: Retired and living in Laindon

Geoff has been a member of the Basildon Philatelic Society for over 30 years and has been collecting stamps for a total of 42 years. He tells me how like many young children he had a stamp collection, and that his interest in the subject grew from there.
  "It is a friendly society of which I hold two officer posts"

Twinned Towns

The Twin Town Programme brings together communities throughout the world. There is usually a common link which connects the towns - similarities in population size, geographical position, historical importance or cultural likeness.

Twin Towns are sometimes referred to as 'Friendship Towns' 'Partner Towns' 'Sister Cities' or 'Brother Cities'.

The idea dates back to the year 836 when Paderborn, Germany and Le Mans, France became twinned, albeit unofficially.

There was a big push for town twinning shortly after World War II. It was seen as a way of bringing Europeans closer together in an act of peace and reconciliation. The joining of Coventry (England) and Dresden (Germany) is one such example, both being cities heavily affected by bombings during the conflict.

The twinning of towns in Europe is now supported by the EU (European Union) with Basildon being twinned with Meaux (France) and Heiligenhaus (Germany).

"As a Twinning Association we help any groups who wish to exchange, such as swimming, table tennis, model railways, rugby etc. but our major concern is the Youth Exchanges where traditionally a group of youngsters from local schools are sent to one of the twin towns for a week each year."

Kate Boucher (Basildon Council)

Welcome to BASILDON

Twinned with
Heiligenhaus, Germany
Meaux, France

Meaux

The city of Meaux can be found 25.5 miles east-northeast of the French capital city of Paris. Its inhabitants are called Meldois, and at the last Census in 1999 there were 67,956 of them.

Access to the city can be made by road - on the N3 from Paris - or by train from the 'Paris de l'Est' station. The SNCF service takes approximately 40 minutes, roughly the same as our C2C service from London Fenchurch Street to Basildon. A single ticket on the SNCF costs just €6.85 (£5.46) as opposed to €9.16 (£7.30) on the C2C. *(Ticket prices and exchange rates correct at time of writing)*

Meaux started out as a primitive Gallic city over 2000 years ago and is today one of the few Episcopal cities remaining in France. This means that the church is governed by bishops, and has been since the 4th Century.

The city is best known throughout the world for its locally produced cheese 'Brie de Meaux' and mustard 'Pommery Moutarde de Meaux'.

Brie, possibly the most well-known of all the cheeses to come out of

Welcome to Meaux

The Meaux train station

France, has been given certificate by the French Atlantic Government stating that only two cheeses can be sold under its name: 'Brie de Meaux' and 'Brie de Melun'.

Brie de Meaux, a soft cheese made from cows milk, was once known as the "King's Cheese" a personal favourite of both King Charlemagne and King Henry IV. It later became celebrated as "The King of Cheeses" following the French Revolution when both the upper and lower classes were free to enjoy the local delicacy.

Pommery Moutarde de Meaux is a whole grain mustard which had been served at the tables of French Kings since 1632. The secret recipe, originally belonging to the religious order of Meaux, was in 1760 passed onto the Pommery family who have guarded the secret to this day.

The central focal point of the city is the Saint Etienne Cathedral, a spectacular piece of Gothic architecture built on the site of the original cathedral. It was dedicated to St Etienne in the 9th Century and later

Meaux

destroyed by the Normans during their invasion. The current cathedral took more than three centuries to complete, from 1175 to 1540.

The Peasants Revolt of 1358, known locally as the 'Jacquerie' was led by revolutionary, Guillaume Cale. The uprising was a response to unfair tax rises imposed upon the peasants during the Hundred Years War. On 9th June a battle in Meaux ended in defeat for the peasants, with the nobleman responding by way of a massacre. More than 10,000 peasants were slaughtered and thrown into the River Marne.

Inside the cathedral there are collections of art work, sculptures, monuments and stain glass windows, plus several designated areas for worship. The tombstone of Jacques Bénigne Bossuet, Bishop of Meaux (1681-1704) is also kept in the cathedral.

Jacques Bénigne Bossuet became the Bishop of Meaux in 1681 and remained so until his death on 12th April 1704. Nicknamed the 'Aigle de Meaux' or 'Eagle of Meaux' Bossuet was a Theologian and Orator who famously made the argument that "government was divine and that kings received their powers from God". The Catholic Encyclopaedia (1913) described Bossuet as being the "greatest pulpit orator of all time". He is now largely remembered for his literacy works, and is famously quoted as saying:

"The greatest weakness of all weaknesses is to fear too much to appear weak"

Beside the Saint-Etienne Cathedral is the Bossuet Museum. In what was once the Bishop's Palace (Palais Episcopal) the museum is now filled with artefacts, sculptures and paintings, most of which relate directly to either JB Bossuet or the history of Meaux.

To the rear of the Museum is the Bossuet Gardens (Jardin Bossuet). Plants and flowers arranged in the shape of a mitre (ceremonial head-dress of bishops) with the centre piece water feature, all designed by the famous landscape gardener André Le Nôtre in the 17th Century. The garden plays host to another of the city's famous residents the 'Aigle de Meaux' – a new variety of rose, one which is slightly purple in colour.

In the late 50's / early 60's large blocks of flats were built in the Pierre Collinet District and Beauval Priority Development area (ZUP) of the city. At the time these residential blocks were considered to be a leading example of modern architecture and seen as a token of success for the city. However today, much like our very own 1960's structures - namely Brooke House, the public opinion of such dwellings has become far less favourable.

Each year, between the months of June to September the Palace courtyard becomes the arena for the 'Meaux Grand Spectacle Historique', A 90 minute performance highlighting the history of the city and performed by a local cast of more than 500 volunteer 'Meldois'
    Visitors are treated to an array of special effects, fireworks and lasers, as well as a phenomenal 3600 spectacular costumes on display.

Jacques Bénigne Bossuet

Profiles

William Corriger

"I have lived in Meaux for 22 years but at the moment I am living in Brazil. I like the geographical situation of Meaux it is right next to Paris but far enough out for there to be countryside when you go out of the town. There are a number of activities for young people (for example a program exists to help you go on free holidays, you just have to work a few hours for the city and then you will be given money to travel with your friends) The most famous thing about Meaux has to be Brie, thanks to the cheese the city is known. There are good job opportunities in the area with Disneyland, one of the most important employers of the area being very close by. However there is a distinct lack of night life in Meaux.

A few years ago I was a part of the exchange program between Basildon, Meaux and Heiligenhaus and was given the chance to visit Basildon. I had a great time there"

Lin Alexandre

"I've lived here for 10 years, It is a very cosmopolitan place, especially in the heart of Meaux, where you can find all kind of activities, for example – the picture house, Museum, beautiful landscapes, a diversity of districts, many gorgeous places - Marne's edge , a lot of cultural places, like the very big library we have , some places to dance and a lot of pubs ...

The " Muzik'elles " which set up in September is very popular now and even Micky Green came to sing there once."

Benjamin Levy

"I have lived in Meaux for 26 years and would say that it is our cathedral which I am most proud of. Meaux is not a very exciting town and I feel that there are very few activities for the people who live here to do. I would recommend to anyone thinking of visiting the city to go see the Cathedral, the Bossuet garden, take a walk along the River Marne, have a drink in one of the pubs and off course see the historical show."

Deborah Nomed

"I have lived in Meaux for 20 years and moved to Dublin (Ireland) 3 years ago. I like the fact that the town is big enough to do different things, though not huge... and very close to Paris! Although after a while, it seems that you've seen everything... And without a car u can't do much after 8pm

I like the festivals, and the contrast between the real urban part and the more quiet part (along the canal or the Marne)

Depeche Mode play cool music, it's amazing they come from the town twinned with Meaux!"

Heiligenhaus

Heiligenhaus is situated in the German State of North Rhine-Westphalia. Three cities – Essen (21km), Wuppertal (31km) and Dusseldorf (23km) – form a triangle around the town.

The town can be reached by road, via the A44, from either Essen or Dusseldorf. Or by public transport, taking the train from Essen or Dusseldorf to Hösel (approx. 20 mins, €4.30) and then from Hösel by bus to Heiligenhaus (approx. 10 mins, €2.30)

(Ticket prices and exchange rates correct at time of writing)

With 70% of the towns area (27km²) being made up of fields and woodlands, Heiligenhaus is very much part of the countryside. They have a total population of just 27,015 and the official motto 'Stadt im Grunen' translates literally into English to 'a town in the Green'.

The coat of arms shows a hammer crossed with a pair of tongs, set above an anvil. These objects are said to symbolise the town's once thriving metal manufacturing industry.

Heiligenhaus translated into English means 'Holy House'. The name is thought to have been taken from a chapel 'Hubertus-Kappele' where the sacred 'holy house' was kept on Hauptsraße in the centre of the town. It was built in the 15th century and subsequently destroyed in 1823. A bronze plaque was installed in 1997 to mark the spot where the chapel once stood.

Heiligenhaus, twinned with…

The bronze plaque

The town has a range of activities available for its residents. There are two Astroturf pitches, swimming pools, tennis courts, 2 golf courses (18 hole), horse-back riding farm stead's and over 45km of hiking and mountain biking trails. In addition to all this there are over 100 active clubs of both a sporting and non-sporting nature.

At number 16 Hüslebecker Straße is 'Der Club'. By day it is a centre for culture and leisure, specifically set up to accommodate the town's youth. By night, on specific dates, it becomes a venue for both home grown and international music acts.

The picturesque and historic area of the town known as Abtsküche is home to two museums. *The Museum of Volunteer Fire-fighters* exhibits a collection which documents over 100 years of fire department history. *The Abtsküche Museum* opened in 1975 looks back on the rural and traditional lives of the town's people.

Beside the remains of the old St Jakobs Chapel and Corn Mill lies the

Abtskücher Stauteich - a large pond which is home to a varied selection of native wildlife including otters, coypu (very large rats), frogs, fish, bats, turtles, wild geese, swans, herons and several other variations of water bird.

Dr Jan Volker Heinisch was born in Dusseldorf in 1976. On the 26th September 2004, aged just 28 years old, he succeeded Herr Peter Ihle to become the Mayor of Heiligenhaus making him the youngest person ever to hold such a position within the state of North West-Westphalia.

During the 1960's, in the areas now known as Unterlip and Oberlip, large residential tower blocks were built. These estates tend to now be populated by lower income families, many of whom are originally from Turkish and Moroccan descent. It was suggested to me that there is little in the way of social integration between the different nationalities, and some believe that this is the cause of many problems.

The manufacturing industry is the town's main employer. However over the past 20 years many of the larger companies have, for a number of reasons, relocated away from the town or suffered bankruptcy. Several companies do remain and with the improvements to the town's infrastructure, put in place by Mayor Heinisch, the economic future of Heiligenhaus is starting to again look more promising.

Town Trivia - Native of Heiligenhaus, Ernst J. Steinbeck, was the father of the American writer John Steinbeck, who went on to become the Pulitzer Prize winning author of classics such as 'Grapes of Wrath' and 'Of Mice and Men'.

The Abtskücher Stauteich

Heiligenhaus Town Hall

Profiles

Nana Woywod

"I attend the "Gesamtschule Heiligenhaus" (Comprehensive School) in Heiligenhaus.

I like that everything in the town is so near together but the people here can be quite unfriendly.

We have a club that's called "Der Club". At day time it's a place where you can hang out and play billiards and at night time it turns into a quite famous live music club with international artists!

Heiligenhaus is quite pretty and in the Spring time everything is green!"

Volker Sternemann

"I used to live in Heiligenhaus between 1984 and 1995 and worked for the town council of Heiligenhaus between 1991 and 2006

I travelled to Meaux (the other twin town) once when I was a school boy with my band, a dixie-jazz-band called "Sir Arthur Crawford's Blech & Blue Small Band". We were invited by the cultural department of Heiligenhaus to play at a big fair which took place somewhere near Meaux.

I also visited Basildon a couple of times, staying in Pitsea - I loved it there! There was a time when I wanted to move to Basildon, work there, settle down and stuff like that. Well, I never did unfortunately and ended up staying in Heiligenhaus."

Mirko Pilger

"I've lived in Heiligenhaus for about twelve years now and grew up in a nearby city named Velbert.

I think the geographical location of Heiligenhaus at the edge of the Ruhr Valley is its biggest advantage. Although the town is very close to the most populated and industrialized region of Germany it's still possible to take long walks in the fields and woods for hours."

The Other Basildon… in Berkshire.

Although not officially linked to Basildon in Essex, the two places are clearly connected by their name.

Basildon, Berkshire is made up of two villages - Upper Basildon, which consists of The Primary School, Village Hall, St Stephens Church and two pubs (the Beehive and Red Lion) and Lower Basildon, which has The Old School, St Bartholomew's Church and a Bangladeshi restaurant called The Tamarind Tree.

In between Upper and Lower Basildon is the National Park Trust property - Basildon Park - a large 18th century, grade I listed, Palladian design Georgian mansion surrounded by magnificent gardens and parklands.

The manor house was built between 1777 and 1783 for Sir Francis Sykes by architect John Carr of York. Sir Francis and his son, the 2nd Baronet, both died within a few months of each other which meant that everything they had was left to the five year old, Francis William Sykes. The grandson of the original owner of Basildon Park grew up to be quite reckless with money, and it wasn't long before he had squandered his inherited fortune and was forced to sell the estate.

Sir Francis William publicly humiliated and disowned his wife after discovering that she had been having an affair with the Irish painter, Daniel Malise. The best friend of Daniel Malise happened to be 'perhaps the most famous of all English authors' Charles Dickens, who at the time was in the process of writing his second novel, Oliver Twist. In response to the manner in which Sir Francis William behaved towards his ex-wife and Daniel Malise, Dickens named the villainous character in his upcoming book 'Bill Sykes' as an act of reprisal.

Basildon Park

The Basildon Park estate was bought for £97,000 by James Morrison, who was known as "the wealthiest commoner in the UK". A self made millionaire who worked to the adage of "small profits and quick return". A famous example of his shrewd business mind and money making ability dates back to 1818, when he noticed that Queen Charlotte was not looking particularly well. He went about buying up all the black crepe he could find and stock piled it. As he predicted the Queen died shortly after and the country went into mourning. In those times, black crepe was the must have accessory when mourning the death of a monarch, and James Morrison was now the countries biggest supplier.

The estate was eventually passed down to James' grandson, Major James Archibald Morrison. The Major was hosting a 'shooting party' at Basildon Park in 1911, when amongst the guest were a group of directors from a printing company. The directors were in the process of deciding a name for their latest range of 'high quality writing paper' and chose to name it after the house in which they were staying, thus the birth of 'Basildon Bond'.

Major Morrison sold the estate to Sir Edward Mauger Iliffe (1st Lord Iliffe) in 1929 for £90,000. Sir Edward went on to auction off much of the parish and sold Basildon Park to a Mr George Samuel Fernando. Mr. Fernando himself then tried to sell on parts of his investment but was unable to find a buyer for the mansion house. However he did sell some of the house's contents (wall fittings, ceilings and furniture) to the Waldorf Astoria Hotel in New York. The pieces remain there to this day, in the 'Basildon Room' Banquet and Conference suite on the 3rd floor.

During both the World Wars the house was requisitioned (taken over) for use by the military. Troops and prisoners both stayed in the house until the end of the conflicts when the Fernando Family were handed back the property. The cost to repair the building proved too expensive, so they sold the mansion to the 2nd Lord Iliffe. The new owner restored the interiors using fittings from other buildings by the original architect, which he gathered from various locations around the country.

The house is full of quality pieces of artwork and furniture. On the wall, in the bedroom of Lady Ifille, are the designs/studies of a 78 feet tapestry which hangs in the Coventry Cathedral, created by Graham Sutherland. The Cathedral was completed in 1962 to replace the original, which was destroyed by bombings during WWII. It became the most famous work of celebrated modern architect, Sir Basil Spence, who also designed and built Basildon's very own Brooke House.

Basildon Park has been the location for two big budget blockbuster movies – Marie Antoinette (2006) directed by Sofia Coppola and starring Kirsten Dunst – and the movie adaptation of the Jane Austin novel 'Pride and Prejudice' (2005) starring Keira Knightly, Donald Sutherland, Matthew MacFadyen and Dame Judy Dench.

Basildon, Berkshire is famous for more than just Basildon Park. The 17th century agriculturalist, Jethro Tull, was born in the parish in 1674 and is buried at St Bartholomew's church in Lower Basildon. He is credited with the invention of the seed drill and horse drawn hoe and is considered by many as being very influential in the progression of 'productive modern agriculture'. A British rock group who formed in the late 60's, also took on the name, Jethro Tull, for their band, and have sold over 60 million albums worldwide.

Resident Profiles

George Bell

"I have lived in Basildon for 17 years. I like the rural aspects, the woods etc but feel that the transport links are poor which makes life difficult for those unable to drive. Pangbourne and Reading are close by and there is plenty to do at both places."

Louisa Stevenson-Hamilton

"I have lived in Basildon for just under 14 years and love it. The best part for me is probably all the footpaths and bridle paths around as these are good for walking the dog! I also like the new renovated playground although it would be nice if there were more things for teenagers like me and my brother. There is a tennis court, garage selling essentials and a playground... but that's pretty much it."

Places of Interest

If asked "What is there to do in Basildon?" most people would answer "Go shopping during the day and onto Bas Vegas at night."

Basildon does have a huge selection of shopping opportunities, with the Town Centre, Eastgate Shopping Centre and Westgate Park all in close proximity. As well as the edge of town shopping areas - The Heron Retail Park and Mayflower Retail Park, which host some of the larger electronical and furniture stores.

The Festival Leisure Park, affectionately nicknamed 'Bas Vegas' by locals, has been the area's main source of entertainment since 1997. "Essex's number 1 leisure destination" hosts a variety of restaurants, bars and nightclubs. As well as a 12 screen cinema, 26 lanes of ten pin bowling, video game areas, two large fully equip fitness centres and a hotel.

However, these are not the only things to do in Basildon. There are many permanent attractions and several annual or occasional ones (Basildon Festival, Essex Country Fair) to keep the people of Basildon thoroughly entertained.

For regular updates of "What's On" in Basildon check the Basildon District website or local newspapers regularly for updates.

This section of the book takes a look at a few of those 'Things to See and Do' found throughout the area.

Barleylands

The Barleylands Farm Centre, Craft Village and Show Grounds have received a major facelift in recent years, making it now one of the areas biggest attractions with *"lots to see and do ALL year round!"*

A gentleman name John Berley farmed the land in 1355 AD and it is thought that this is where the name Barleylands originates from.

In 1968 the land was bought by the Philpot family who continue to run the farm to this day.

The Farm Centre is where children can meet and feed various farm animals. They can also take part in a range of fun activities - tractor and trailer rides, miniature railway, straw bale maze, designated petting area and an adventure playground. There is also a newly built Discovery Centre where displays and interactive games teach the children about the farm, its owners, the countryside, where food comes from and how it is produced.

The Craft Village plays host to numerous commercial and artistic outlets including glass blowers, blacksmiths, cake decorators, florists, potters and painters plus many more. There is also a choice of two eateries, the Magic Mushroom Restaurant and the Hive Tea Rooms which serve a mouth watering selection of locally grown fresh produce.

In addition to weekly car boot sales (weather permitting) and twice

Barleylands

monthly farmers market, The Barleylands calendar is packed full of events held throughout the year.

In June, the South East Essex Garden Show is in town, with over 120,000m^2 of plants, crafts, food, drink and an ice skating rink.

September 2008 saw the 22nd Essex Country Show at Barleylands, attracting approximately 35,000 visitors over the two days. Displays of steam engines, tractors, vintage cars and motor boats can be found alongside over 200 craft and trade stalls.

As well as helicopter rides, puppet shows, a sheep show, a birds of prey demonstration and a fairground there was a special performance by the Imps Motorcycle Display Team with youngsters aged between 5 and 16 put on a show of synchronised riding skills.

Opening times at Barleylands vary depending on the time of year. For more information, plus a full list of upcoming events, go to www.barleylands.co.uk or call 01268 290229

Cater Museum

The premises of 74 High Street, Billericay play host to the Cater Museum. The last people to live at the address were Mr & Mrs Eales. Fred Eales was a harness maker by trade and Mrs Eales looked after kennels for stray dogs.

The property was later purchased by Mrs A.M. Cater who in memory of her husband, William Alexander Cater, gifted the premises and much of its contents to the people of Billericay in the form of a museum in 1960.

The museum displays a vast collection of relics and memorabilia relating to the town and its history. Old photos of the town and its people line the walls of the 3 storey building. There are 6 rooms of exhibits and each of the rooms has its own theme, one room on the upper floor is dedicated to 'Billericay at War' with many items of interest including an RAF Lancaster bomber's emergency liquid compass and a piece of a Nazi war plane, which in 1940, had crash landed in the town. There is also a Victorian style bedroom, kitchen and Parlour on the 2nd floor which contains many items you would have found in a home of the late 1800's.

There are also Roman and Bronze Age relics as well as fragments of medieval pottery on show, some of which were found locally in the town. One of the oddest pieces is a preserved two headed lamb, which was born on a Billericay farm and lived for just 6 weeks.

Cater Museum

Heritage Lottery Funded money was recently put towards restoring the garden to its historical appearance, with all 20th century concrete rendering being replaced by materials that would have been used by the original builders. The installation of a virtual tour allows those unable to climbs the stairs, to view some of the artefacts on a video screen located on the ground floor.

During the refurbishment of a garden wall, volunteers found six crates of artefacts, believed to have belonged to Mr and Mr Eales. Amongst the find were Victorian pipes, ginger beer jars and medicine bottles containing liquid.

The museum is opened Monday to Saturday from 2pm-5pm and admission is free. More information can be found on their website www.catermuseum.co.uk

Motorboat Museum

When opened in 1986, the Motorboat Museum became the only public museum of its kind. Starting off with just five boats on loan, the museum now describes itself as being "Britain's foremost collection of sporting and leisure motorboats and engines" It displays a timeline of motorboating history, from the early steam powered craft of the 19th century right up to the ultra modern vessels of the present day.

Amongst the many exhibits on display is the 'Defender II' a racing boat dating back to 1909, plus the 'Steam Launch Cygnet' which is the oldest piece in the collection, having been built in 1873. Also on display is the 'Fairy Huntress' which was used in the filming of the James Bond movie, 'From Russia With Love' and the 'Miss Britain IV' which held the world water speed record back in the 1980s.

Inside the museum there is opportunity for children, and adults, to play with the remote control miniature boats (20p) and at the rear of the museum there is a 30m x 35m model boat pond and home to the Wat Tyler Model Boat Club. The club are always on the look out for new members and meet twice a month on a Sunday. *Contact the museum reception for more information.*

The museum is open 5 days a week (closed Tuesday and Wednesday, except on school holidays when the museum is opened 7 days) Opening

Motorboat Museum

times are between 10am – 4pm and admission and parking are both free.

If you want to find out more before you visit then log on to the new website - www.motorboatmuseum.org.uk

Inside the museum

Plotland Museum

In the early 1900s, many Londoners fulfilled their dreams of owning their own weekend retreats, by buying up plots of land in the Essex countryside. The farmland of Dunton was a particularly popular location. When war broke out in 1939, many Londoners moved to the area permanently and set up home in their holiday dwellings, away from the frequently bombed target of the capital city. The area quickly became populated with a total of around 200 homes, known locally as 'Gumboot Hill' or 'Dodge City'.

After the war, the New Town of Basildon was created and all but a few of the Plotland homes were either destroyed or left to ruin. One of these rare surviving buildings 'The Haven', a bungalow on Third Avenue, is open to the public and offers an insight into the life of the early 'Plotlanders'.

The plot of land where 'The Haven' stands was bought by a Mr Fredrick Mills back in 1933 for just £20. Mr Mills was a carpenter and built the home over a period of a few years. Three generations of the Mills family went on to live in the house, right up until 1975. The Haven is now part of the Plotlands Walk, a 1.4km trial which is habitat for a variety of the Nature Reserves wildlife. On a clear day, impressive views

The Haven

of the city of London skyline can be seen from certain points along the walk.

The bungalow has been set up to look just as it would have done back in the 1930s/40s, and is fully kitted out with all authentic furniture, ornaments and appliances.

The Plotland trial can be found on Third Avenue, off of Lower Dunton Road, as part of the Langdon Nature Reserve, which is owned by the Essex Wildlife Trust. It is open from 9am - 5pm, Tuesday to Sunday and on Bank Holiday Mondays.

More information can be found on the website www.essexwt.org.uk

The kitchen of 'The Haven', Third Avenue

Towngate Theatre

In 1968 the original Towngate Theatre was opened by Lord Goodman, who at the time was the Chairman of the Arts Council for Great Britain.

The new Towngate Theatre, which remains today, was designed by Renton Howard Wood and Levin. It was opened by actress Kate O'Mara on 23rd April 1988 and was described by the Eastern Arts Association as "the jewel in the crown for Essex".

Within the first few months of opening, the theatre hosted a performance of the Shakespeare comedy - As You Like It', renditions of the musicals - 'West Side Story' *and* 'Joseph and the Amazing Technicolor Dreamcoat' as well as appearances by comedians Hale and Pace and cockney songsters Chas & Dave.

The design of the main auditorium was based upon that of a classic Georgian playhouse with the seats arranged on three levels – The stalls, the dress circle and upper circle. The main theatre can accommodate 542 people (seated) and 775 (standing) with the Mirren Studio, named after Essex actress Helen Mirren, comfortably holding up to 180. The theatre has 2 bars, 2 large foyers plus the facilities to cater for business conferences or seminars.

The Towngate continues to provide the venue for performances put on by many of the school and amateur dramatics groups of the town.

Towngate Theatre

The theatre is currently recruiting people to volunteer their time to assist these local groups stage their productions and/or help their front of house team. If interested then please email your name and contact details to towngate@basildon.gov.uk

The theatre is open from 9am to 5pm (Monday - Friday) and from 1 hour before the start of a performance in the evening and on weekends.

For more information and to find out 'What's On' you can visit the website www.basildon.gov.uk or call 01268 465465

Art & Sculptures

Throughout the town there are many fine examples of art and sculpture. Some of which were created by the countries leading and most successful artists. This chapter takes a look at the works of these people. As members of the general public, we often walk past without noticing or appreciating just how much time, effort and skill was required in making these pieces.

Mother and Child Statue

Costing £4,000 back in 1961, this bronze statue was built to symbolise the growth of Basildon New Town. It was created by the sculptor, Maurice Lambert (1901-1964) who has a collection of his work displayed at the National Portrait Gallery.

Tenor Clef

On the side of Freedom House this cast aluminium sculpture with stainless steel wires was designed by A.J. Poole and erected in 1960.

Mother and Child statue

Brooke House

"84 flats separated into 14 floors and held up by eight 'V' shaped concrete posts". This grade II listed building is considered by some, to be an architectural masterpiece and by others, an outdated eyesore.

The controversial dwellings were designed by Sir Basil Spence who also designed the Coventry Cathedral. The building took its name from the former housing minister, Henry Brooke, and when opened on July 1962 it became home to many of the business managers and directors working in the area at the time.

Brooke House and Tenor Clef

Bus Station Mosaic

Designed by John Gordon, this 96m x 4m (315 x 13ft) mosaic time line is made up of 16,000 tiles, all of which were hand painted.

St Martins Bell Tower

Opened by Queen Elizabeth II on 12th March 1999. The tower comprises of 6 bells, housed inside an 85ft octagonal spire, and made up from 300 square metres of glass.

Not only is it the first glass and steel Bell Tower in the world, but also, one of its bells - The Tenor bell, was the first ever to be cast by a woman (Joanne Hille in 1441).

Bus Station Mosaic

Sundial

Out the front of the Towngate Theatre is a sundial built into the floor, this was designed by Tam Giles and constructed in 1997. Just over 10 years later and the whole paved area is uneven and in dire need of being dug up and re-laid.

Woodman

Some say that this was commissioned because of complaints made to the council claiming that the 'Mother & Child fountain' brought attention to the fact that there is a notably high number of single parent families in the town. The woodman is said to have been brought in as the father figure to the family unit.

Created by local sculpture, Dave Chappele, he would publicly carve the piece amongst the crowds of shoppers in the town centre. Due to weather damage the woodman is to be taken down, treated and moved to a new location (possibly Wat Tyler Park).

The Bailor Christ

When first designed in 1968 by Mr T.B. Huxley-Jones and placed above the porch of St Martins Church, this statue caused major controversy because of its unusual portrayal of Jesus Christ.

This proved to be the Sculptors final piece of work. Just a few months after its completion the artist was admitted to St Johns Hospital, Chelmsford with a heart condition, Four days later he died on 10th December 1968.

His other works include several sculpture heads/busts which can be seen in his book 'Modelled Portrait Heads' (Scopas Handbooks

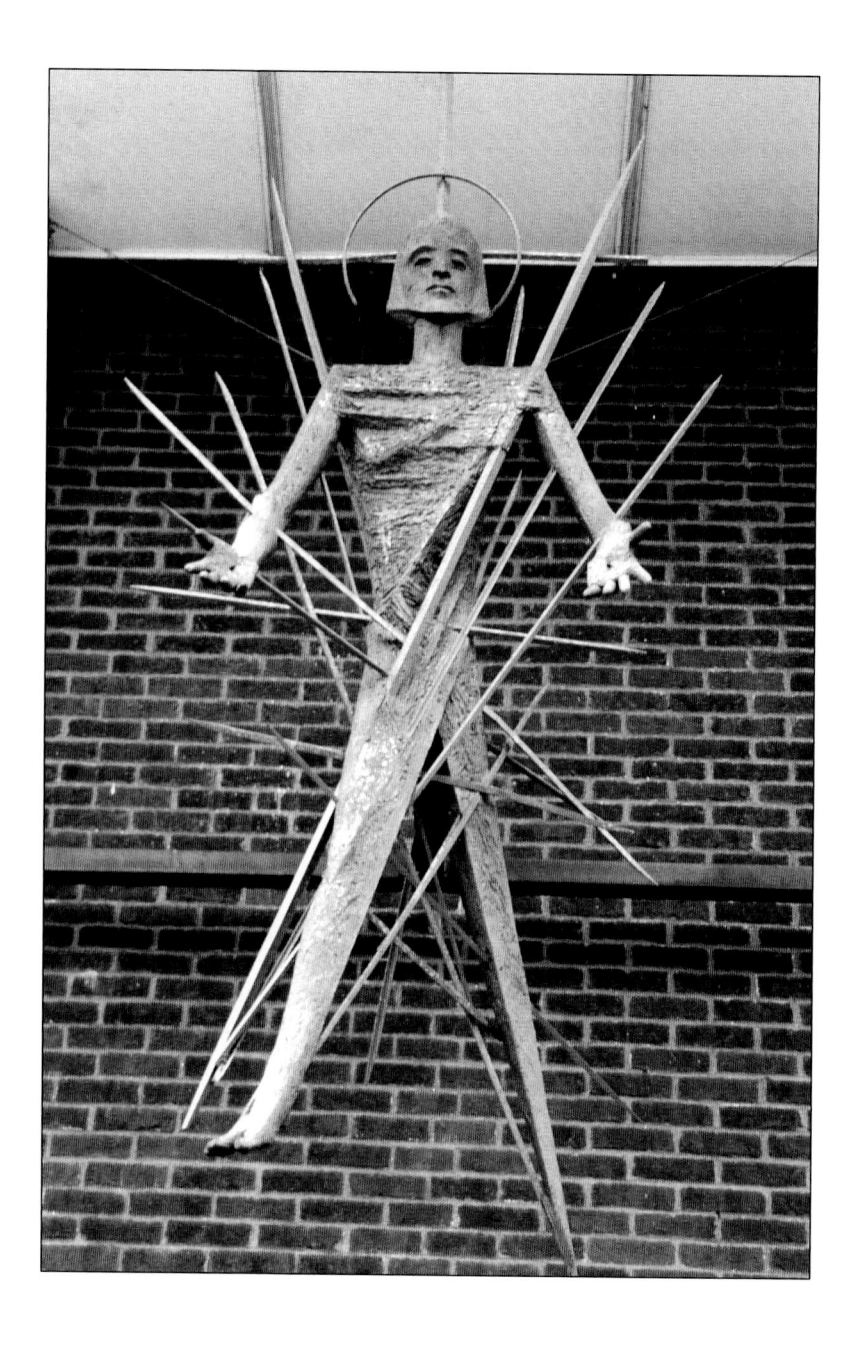

The Bailor Christ

1960) Possibly his most famous sculpture being a statue of the Greek Sun God – Helios, which could be found in the central garden of the BBC Television and News building at Woodlane, Shepherds Bush, London.

Cats Cradle Pussiwillow III Clock

Created by Rowland Emett in 1981. It was unveiled at its original location, outside Savacentre in the Eastgate centre, by ex-Goon Michael Bertine. There are a few similar art pieces throughout the country all designed by Emett, but it will be his creation of the 'Chitty Chitty Bang Bang' car, that he will be most remembered for.

The clock is supposed to chime with its pieces rotating and spinning every hour but hasn't for some time.

Pineapple – Trafford House

This Corten metal fountain was designed by William Mitchell. Corten metal goes rusty or oxidises in a controlled way. So when water is activated, each 'triangle' dripped and turned deep red, as was the sculptures intention.

Toblerone, Ghyllgrove

This unusually shaped building was transported to Basildon from Sweden. Based on the Scandinavian, 'Potten A Frame' design, it was officially opened on 1st November 1983 by Lord Len Murray. The now named 'Basildon Community Resource Centre' is a registered charity which gives assistance to the homeless and unemployed individuals/families in the district.

Homer

This bronze statue of "a squatting poet with a dove on its shoulder and a lyre on one arm" has been moved many times around the town. I have memories as a child of it being upstairs in the Towngate Theatre, usually with a cigarette butt positioned on the dove's beak. It has since then been on display at the Eastgate Management Centre and in the foyer of Brooke House. At the moment the whereabouts are unknown?

Commissioned in 1960, and costing around £2,000, the sculpture by Mr S.E. McWilliam was given to the town as a gift from Liverpool MP Mr Harold Lever.

Wendy Taylor CBE

Artist/Sculpture, Wendy Taylor CBE, has a number of her works on display around Basildon.

Born in Stamford, Lincolnshire but raised nearby in Bow, East London. Wendy is famed for being one of the first artists "to take art out of the galleries and into the streets" It is possible that there is more of Wendy's work on permanent display in Britain than that of any other living artist.

Compass Bowl (1980)

Located behind 'Toys r Us', in the centre of the roundabout on Southernhay. This largely landscaping project, lead the way for Wendy being considered for other projects in the area.

After seeing a recent picture of the area Wendy declared *"What a pity, so sadly neglected now"*

Roundacre (1985-1990)

The original roundabout, built in 1958 was feeling the strain of rush hour traffic so the Basildon Development Corporation decided to reshape the area with 2 roundabouts and a short dual carriage to connect them.

The project was separated into Phase I (1985-1988) and Phase II (1989-1990). Phase I was made up of 3 large subways, footpaths, cycle paths and a new road bridge. Phase II included more underpasses, tiling designs, paving layout, landscaping and the precast Animal Fresco.

The Animal Fresco is an underpass made up of concrete panels showing life size silhouettes of animals (including an Elephant, a Camel and a Kangaroo) all seen to be running towards the park. At the opposite end of the underpasses Gloucester Park entrance is a cobbled mosaic set in concrete of a Tortoise and a Rhinoceros.

Wendy completely redesigned the shape of the underpasses in the area; some will remember the old square box shaped subway which preceded the current layout. The new design was more spacious, better lit and safer. She took out the vertical walls where 'would be attackers' could push victims up against and replaced them with a curved design.

Animal Subway – Roundacre

Armillary Sundial (1989-1990)

The ornamental time piece can be found in the centre of Roundacre's southern roundabout.

Upon seeing recent photographs, Wendy acknowledged that *"The Armillary Sundial has appeared to have grown two weird props for health and safety reasons, very depressing"*

Some other examples of Wendy's work:
Timepiece - 1973 - St Katherines Dock, Tower Hill, London
Anchor Iron - 2004 - Anchor Iron Wharf, London
Tortoises with Triangle and Time - 2000 - Holland Park, London

More information can be found at www.wendytaylorsculpture.co.uk or the Edward Lucie-Smith book called - 'Wendy Taylor' published by Arts Books International (1992)

Armillary Sundial

Pubs of Basildon

The oldest pubs in Basildon are the Five Bells in Vange and the Crown (now Harvester) in Langdon Hills.

The building which houses the Harvester (previously The Crown) dates back to 1856. The land was once owned by the Crown (the Monarchy) which is where the name of the public house came about. The Crown Pub was once the meeting place for hunting activities as well as being a site for pigeon shooting. Many of the Irish settlers to the area would gather in the car park and listen to radio transmissions of the Gaelic Football and Hurling finals. Being the 2nd highest point in Essex it was the only place that they could pick up a clear reception.

The first recorded landlord of the Five Bells public house was William West around the time of 1769, although the deeds of the house go back as far as 1690. The pub lies to the west of the Five Bells roundabout which was once a field called 'Crouchmans' or 'Bell Field'.

'Pub Culture' is an important part of British heritage; however throughout the country local public houses are closing down at the alarming rate of nearly 5 a day *(figure taken from research made by the British and Beer Pub Association (BBPA) in 2008).*

The cheap supermarket sales of alcohol, the rise in home computers (internet access), games consoles and numerous television channels as well as the smoking ban have all contributed to the decline of pub attendances here in the UK.

Many pubs are forced to close down because the land on which the properties stand is, when sold to a property developer, worth substantially more than could ever be made through profit as a public house.

There have been several examples of this right here in Basildon. The Fortune of War, The Commodore, The Powerhouse (previously The Bull), The Jolly Cricketers, St Basils Social, The Irish Club (Essex Country Club) and The Double Six have all been replaced by newly built residential areas. It looks likely that more will follow suit in the coming years with the ongoing future of the Winston Social Club looking uncertain.

There are also a few pubs which have closed and been left unoccupied for a considerable time. The Oasis, Cahoots (previously Yates) and The Railway have been boarded up and seeming left for ruin. Whether these pubs will ever reopen again remains to be seen.

Drinker's Profiles

Drew Walsh

I have been drinking in Basildon for fifteen years now and have noticed the drinking culture change a lot in that time. Before pub goers were happy just to drink beer, but nowadays people drink a lot more shots and weird and wonderful drinks which I imagine they have discovered overseas.

In terms of the cost, ten years ago you would quite easily come home with change from £30 but these days it is more like £70 which is far in advance of the rate of inflation.

Back in the day the best 'Club' was Time Discotheque it was quite cheap to drink in there, especially on a Thursday night. Before Time we would drink in The Moon on the Square because it was just 99p for a bottle of Becks.

The Gun public house

Boarded up - The Oasis

Nowadays there are far more of the so-called 'trendy' bars which charge an arm and a leg for a drink. Pubs like the Moon on the Square still are still around but tend to attract an older clientele with youngsters more likely to frequent the Sports Bars.

Moving forward I can see doom and gloom for pubs, especially with the current financial climate as it is. People are beginning to 'watch' the pennies and this will have a direct impact on Pubs and Clubs.

Steven Bowler

I've been drinking in Basildon for 11 years or so and to be honest for a town of its size it has a disappointing array of watering holes.

The thing that is totally shocking about drinking in Basildon is the prices. London and local prices are so similar now that going into the city for a few just isn't a big deal anymore. When I was 18 I would go out with £40 have a great night and still have money left over for a curry, cheese and chips from Tony Dow's on the way home. It costs over twice as much to go out now and I put it down to greed on behalf of the local night spots who will charge £4 for a bottle and still make you pay anywhere up to £8 just to get in.

Popular Culture

There are a number of the towns' residents, both current and previous, who have achieved notable success and recognition in the genres of either music, film, TV, sports or business. Many of whom were kind enough to spare me a little of their time to answer my questions.

This section looks closely at the careers and achievements of those people, and reveals details of their connection and relationship with Basildon.

In addition to the profiles of famous and successful "Basildonians", this section also looks at references to Basildon made in TV, Film, Literature and advertising, as well as times when the town was used as the setting for media productions and events.

Depeche Mode

The story of Depeche Mode begins in the late 70's. Vince Clarke (who at the time was still using his original name - Vince Martin) and Andrew Fletcher formed a friendship as members of the 5th Basildon Boys Brigade. Meetings were held at Janet Duke Primary School (Markhams Chase) before moving to nearby St Pauls Methodist Church (Ballards Walk). It was there that they formed their first band named 'No Romance in China', Vince was lead guitarist and vocalist, Andrew played bass with Sue Padgett on guitar and Pete Hobbs on drums. They only played in public once, on a Wednesday night at the Double Six Public House, Whitmore Way.

Vince was a pupil at Laindon School, High Road, and Fletcher was attending St Nicholas Comprehensive (now James Hornsby School). It was at the latter where Fletch became friends with another young budding musician, Martin Gore. Martin was playing in a band called 'Norman and the Worms' together with Phil Burnett and Pete Hobbs. Norman and the Worms achieved slightly more longevity than 'No Romance in China' with them taking part in the Basildon Rock Festival, held at the Bandstand in Gloucester Park. The band also entered a talent contest hosted by the Castlemayne Pub, where they lost out on first prize to a Tom Jones impersonator.

Vince and Fletch then formed the duo 'Composition of Sound' which they later turned into a three piece by asking Martin to join. Together they decided that they were not very good with guitars and opted instead for synthesisers.

Deb Dandnay, who later became a girlfriend of Vince, was having a leaving party at the Paddocks Community Centre, Laindon on 30th May 1980 before heading off to work at Butlins Holiday Camp for the summer. Composition of Sound secured their debut gig at the party with a line up of Vince on lead vocals and 'synth', Martin on 'synth' and backing vocals, Fletch playing the bass and Rob Andrews (a neighbour and lifelong friend of Andrew Fletcher) on drum machine.

The bill was shared with another local band, French Look, featuring Robert Marlow (who later became known as Rob Allen), Paul Redmond

Martin Gore on stage

and none other than Martin Gore! Drum machines and synthesisers were relatively rare in Basildon at this time so band members and equipment would often be shared.

Composition of Sound played a couple more gigs with the same line up, the first at Scamps nightclub in Southend and the last at a youth club at Woodlands School with the band performing to a room full of 9 year olds!

The band would sometimes rehearse on weekday evenings, in one of the classrooms at Woodlands School. On one occasion the band 'French Look' was also there. French Look synth player, Paul Redmond, was friends with a lad called Dave Gahan who would mix the sounds for the band. Dave recalls singing a rendition of David Bowies 'Heroes' that night in Woodlands School and being overheard in the other room by Vince. The reason for asking Dave to join Composition of Sound, according to Vince, was that *"no one came to our gigs and with Dave being very, very popular we'd thought we would get him in the band. He really looked the part, so we decided to audition him as the vocalist."*

Dave was a bit of a tearaway, being suspended from Barstable School in his younger days and after several appearances at Juvenile Court, he wound up having to attend a weekend detention centre at a sub-borstal for 1 year. After school he was accepted on a course at Southend College studying 'Retail Display' where an interest in fashion developed.

The first time the Composition of Sound played as a four piece fronted by Dave Gahan, was on June 14th 1980 in the Upper School Cloakroom of St Nicholas Comprehensive School on Leinster Road. Supported by French Look, tickets were sold on the door for 50p. A plaque has been erected in what is now the school Main Hall, in tribute to this momentous moment.

The lack of decent venues in Basildon meant that the band had to search for gigs elsewhere, mainly ending up in Southend. They also played often at what is now known as 'The Pink Toothbrush' in Rayleigh. At the time it was called 'Crocs Glamour Club' named in honour of the live crocodile which was kept in a cage on the premises. The RSPCA eventually put a stop to this, demanding that the creature be moved to a more suitable environment.

Singer Dave Gahan on stage

On October 29th 1980, a gig at Ronnie Scott's Jazz club in London's Soho saw the band ditch the name Composition of Sound in favour of 'Depeche Mode' (the title of a French Fashion magazine which Dave Gahan used to read). The title translated into English means 'Fast Fashion' or 'Hurry up Fashion'

In November of that year Depeche Mode were mentioned for the first time in local Basildon newspaper, Evening Echo. *"Posh clobber could clinch it for Mode – some of these perfumed ponsed up futuristic pop bands don't hold a candle for these four Basildon lads. They are Depeche Mode, who could go a long way if someone just pointed them in the direction of a decent tailor"*

11th November 1980. Depeche Mode played support to a newly signed band on the Mute records label, Fad Gadget, at Bridge House, Canning Town. After the show, label boss Daniel Miller, told the

> **Martin Gore and Andrew Fletcher**
> former students of this school together with
> **Vince Clarke and Dave Gahan**
> played their first concert here in 1980 as
> *Depeche Mode*
> The band have since gone on to sell more than Seventy Million Albums worldwide

Plaque in the main hall of James Hornsby School (previously St Nicholas)

Basildon boys *"Let's put out a single"* and a few months later 'Dreaming of Me' was released peaking at number 57 on the UK singles chart and named "No.1 Independent Single of the Year". Offers came flooding in from major labels but Vince, the bands main songwriter, convinced the others that sticking with Daniel Miller and Mute Records was in all their best interests. There was no official contract and nothing was signed, the costs and profits were just split 50/50 between the band and label.

In addition to several shows lined up in London, the band headlined a gig at Southend College of Technology and played twice more in Basildon, Sweeny's on April 28th and Raquels on May 3rd.

A string of hit singles, including the top ten sensation 'Just Can't Get Enough' propelled the band into the spotlight, with an appearance on BBC's Top of the Pops followed by a 14 date UK tour. Racquels Nightclub, on Market Pavement in Basildon town centre played host to the homecoming leg of the tour, with the boys performing in front of a capacity crowd of adoring local fans.

A fortnight after the tour finished, the band announced the official news that Vince Clarke would no longer be part of Depeche Mode. The reason Vince gave for leaving as not being happy, contented or fulfilled by their success.

The band continued as a three piece. Martin Gore stepped up to take the role of chief songwriter, with classically trained musician, Alan Wilder, brought in to replace Vince.

Alan was originally hired solely as a stand in for the live performances, but remained with the band until 1995. His opinion of Basildon is not a particularly positive one. For nearly 20 years he was part of Basildon's biggest musical export, however he recalls having spent very little time in the town. *"I am pleased to say that my knowledge of Basildon is extremely limited due to the fact that I have only been there about three times. All my visits were early on in my career with Depeche Mode, and at a time when I was really into photography and used to routinely carry around a shoulder bag containing my camera equipment. My overriding memory of Basildon is sitting in a disgusting pub and being told by Daryl Bamonte (roadie to the band) to uncross my legs and hide my shoulder bag or I was likely to get the shit kicked out of me* for being a poof. Nice, eh? I hate it when journalists refer to me as a Basildon Boy."

The band has gone on to achieve global success with a total of 14 top ten UK singles, a string of highly proclaimed albums as well as embarking on several massive world tours including sell out shows at the Pasadena Rose Bowl (LA), The New York Giants Stadium (NY) Los Angeles Dodgers Stadium (LA)

In 2009 the band are set to release their eagerly awaited 12th Studio album. In addition to this Depeche Mode are set to embark on the mammoth "Tour of the Universe" where the band will play to packed out stadiums across the globe, including a UK date at the London O2 Arena.

Julia Tennant 'Depeche Mode - Super Fan'

Julia is originally from New York, but now lives in North Carolina.

I have been a fan of Depeche Mode since I was 14 years old. I bought all of their albums and listened to them over and over again, mesmerized by Dave's deep voice and Martin's ingenious lyrics. I love their music so much that I put their name on my license plate, "DPCHMODE."

I visited Basildon in December 2003 when I was 27 years old. I went their solely because the members of Depeche Mode are from there and I wanted to see where they grew up. It was like a dream come true for me. I remember taking the c2c from Barking and feeling a rush of excitement as we neared Basildon. My friend Andy and I got off at Laindon and walked to the James Hornsby School (formerly the St. Nicholas Comprehensive School) where Martin Gore and Andy Fletcher were once pupils. It is also where Depeche Mode first performed together as a band. As St. Nicholas Church loomed in the distance on the hill, I stood in front of the school and took a photograph, hardly believing where I was. It all seemed surreal. After reading about it for so many years, finally seeing it was so very exciting. I tried to absorb in as much as I could about the town, looking at the scenery and trying to guess which house Dave, Martin, Andy or Vince may have grown up in. We went to the Eastgate centre, a shopping mall with a HMV record store inside. I looked around and my friend Andy chatted with the clerk who, after finding out why I was in Basildon, let me have one of the "Depeche Mode" CD dividers from the rack. He also told us that Dave's mother had been at that record store a few days earlier to buy several copies of his solo release "Paper Monsters". Needless to say, I was in awe.

  I found the people to be friendly and very interested in the fact that I was from America. I was surprised that some people did not even know who Depeche Mode were. I was also surprised that people outside of Basildon (and many who live there) considered it to be less than desirable. Everything I have ever read or heard about Basildon had always been negative but I found it to be a very nice. I really enjoyed myself and not just because Depeche Mode are from there. I would love to visit again one day. My trip to Basildon will always be a very memorable one for me.

Yazoo (Vince Clarke & Alison Moyet)

Following his departure from Depeche Mode, Vince Clarke used his newly found spare time to concentrate on song writing. During this period, an advert in the Melody Maker, placed by fellow Basildonian Alison Moyet caught his attention. Alison was looking to find a "rootsy R&B band" but Vince gave her a call anyway and asked if she would be interested in making a demo of a song he had written.

They formed the duo 'Yazoo' and together with Mute Records released the single 'Only You' on March 15th 1982. The song was a nationwide hit reaching number 2 in the UK charts.

Yazoo made two albums, Upstairs at Eric's (1982) *and* You and Me both (1983) producing a series of hit singles. In 1983 the band picked up a Brit Award for Best British breakthrough act.

Vince and Alison were forced to change the bands name for a scheduled tour in America. A Blues label already held the rights to the title 'Yazoo' so to avoid what was reported in the Evening Echo as being a "£3.5 million Law Suit" they changed the name to 'Yaz'. The record labels copyright only applied to the USA so the name Yazoo remained the same everywhere else.

The band split shortly before the release of the LP 'You and Me Both' in 1983. It would be 25 years later, in 2008, before the band would get

Vince Clarke –
Yazoo

Alison Moyet –
Yazoo

to play those songs live. The pair reunited for a tour of the UK, Europe & America and released a 4 disc box set 'In your Room' which included the two albums (re-mastered) a b-side and remixes album and a DVD featuring promotional videos and an interview.

Vince Clarke
(The Assembly & Erasure)

After success with Depeche Mode and Yazoo, Vince's next project was a one off collaboration with sound engineer and producer, Eric Radcliffe, and ex-Undertones front man, Fergal Sharkey, on vocals. Under the guise of 'The Assembly' they released the single 'Never Never' which reached #4 in the UK charts.

Following this Vince teamed up with Paul Quinn of eighties band 'Bourgie Bourgie' to release 'One Day'. The single failed to make it into the top 75 so Vince placed an advert in Melody Maker looking for a singer. Peterborough born Andy Bell was one of the many to reply and together they formed Erasure with whom Vince achieved the longevity which never came from his other projects.

Erasure have sold over 25 million albums worldwide to date, notched up five consecutive number one albums in the UK and produced a string of Top Ten hit singles. The duo are set to start writing for a new album sometime in 2009 with a release date due shortly after.

Erasure live

Alison Moyet

Alison grew up in Basildon and attended Janet Duke Infant & Junior School, before moving onto St Nicholas Comprehensive (now James Hornsby School), where she was in the same year as Depeche Mode members Martin Gore and Andrew Fletcher.

As part of the rising punk scene in Basildon, Alison formed 'The Vandals' with school friends Kim Forey, Sue Paget and guitarist Robert Allen (Marlow). They performed live for the first time at The Grand Hotel in Leigh on Sea and went on to play many more local gigs including appearances at Van Gogh's in Paycocke Road, Woodlands Youth Centre in Kingswood and at the Bandstand in Gloucester Park.

The band split after just one year and Alison replaced Mike Maynard as the vocalist for 'The Vicars'. During Alison's short time with the band there were some memorable gigs - the Shrimpers Club - the Southend College of Technology, as well as several jam sessions at the Double Six pub (previously on the corner of The Hatherley and Whitmore Way)

Alison went on to start a blues band called 'The Screaming Ab Dabs', but shortly after was approached by Vince Clarke and asked to record a demo of 'Only You' and in doing so formed the hugely successful pop duo 'Yazoo'

Two albums and several hit singles later, Yazoo spilt and Alison reinvented herself as a solo artist. Her first album, entitled 'Alf' was released on 5th November 1984. The album went quadruple platinum, spent a total of two years in the charts and sold over 1.5 million copies in the UK alone.

At the 1985 Brit Awards, Alison picked up the award for Best British Female Solo Artist and the same year appeared on stage twice during the Live Aid Concert alongside Paul Young, Bob Geldof, David Bowie, Pete Townsend and Paul McCartney.

The next studio release 'Raindancing' in 1987 came close to mirroring the phenomenal success of 'Alf' peaking at no.2 in the UK charts and rewarding the singer/songwriter with a second Brit Award for Best British Female Solo Artist.

Alison was not happy with the commercial production of her music, so with her third LP 'Hoodoo' (released in April 1991), she opted for a more "earthier and personal album". The popular media were less enthusiastic about her latest efforts and as a result the LP narrowly missed out on a top ten chart position. In contrast, a single from the album "It Wont Be Long" received a Grammy nomination for Best Female Rock Performer.

In 1994 Alison released the album 'Essex' which would be her last studio recording for over 8 years. She refused to record 'radio friendly pop music' for the sake of chart positions and wanted to be more true to herself and make records closer to the heart and to her musical roots. In August 2002 she was released from her contract with Sony and signed to Sanctuary Records. Her fifth studio album 'Hometime' was released and went Gold, earning Alison nominations for both a Brit Award and The Mercury Prize.

A collection of cover songs released in 2004 entitled 'Voice' was followed in 2007 by the album 'The Turn'. The LP included 3 songs written for the West End stage play 'Smaller' in which Alison worked alongside good friends Dawn French (acting) and Kathy Burke (directing).

Alison was no stranger to the West End having played the part of Matron 'Mama' Morton in the hit musical 'Chicago' back in 2001, alongside fellow Basildonian Denise Van Outen.

After the completion of the 2008 Yazoo Reconnected Tour, Alison hit the road again as a solo artist, completing 16 dates in the US & Canada followed up by a 10 date UK tour in 2009.

Alison Moyet

Keith Chapman

Basildon born Keith Chapman is the creator of children's television programmes - Bob the Builder, Fifi and the Flowertots and Roary the Racing Car. The shows provide entertainment to millions and continue to generate substantial profits from worldwide licensing rights and product sales.

Keith was born in Basildon in 1958 and lived at Waldegrave, Kingswood before moving to Plumberow, Lee Chapel North in 1964. He attended Janet Duke Junior and then went onto St. Nicholas Comprehensive (which is now James Hornsby High School)

Keith, from the age of 12, had a morning paper round; an after school paper round (delivering the Evening Echo) and on Saturday's would work at a newsagent in Laindon shopping centre.

"I had a great group of mates, some I still see, although I wouldn't say I did particularly well at school, apart from art which was the only subject I was interested in. I spent most of my time out in the corridors waiting for the cane or slipper. But in those days kids had real freedom, we would go off all day on adventures. No sitting indoors playing computer games for us, just a football and a sense of fun. I left Basildon for Norfolk when I was 16 to go to Art College. I still have relatives in Basildon and enjoy going back when I can."

"The one thing I did have was fantastic confidence in my ability and a dream that one day I would be rich and successful. I was very, very determined and I never gave up."

The 2008 electoral campaign saw future United States President, Barack Obama adopt the popular slogan "Yes We Can". At the time, many fractions of the media claimed (albeit tongue in cheek) that inspiration may have come from Bob's very own catchphrase "Can we fix it.... Yes we can!"

When asked by Alice Wignall of the Guardian whether he had considered legal action, Keith jokingly replied *"I don't think so. He's got his finger on the nuclear button and the whole of the US army under his command. I don't want Delta Force coming over my garden wall. He's free to use it as much as he likes."*

Bob the Builder

Bob the Builder was launched in 1999 and is now broadcast to over 240 territories and in 45 languages.

Known in France as "*Bob le Bricoleur*", In Germany as "*Bob der*

Baumeister" in Spain as "*Bob y sus amigos*" and Poland as "Bob Budowniczy" There was even a Welsh language version made called "Bob Y Bildar"

The voice of Bob is played by actor Neil Morrissey who as a result of the show has twice topped the UK singles charts. In 2000 'Bob' beat Eminem and Westlife to the Christmas number one slot with 'Can We Fix It?' then again the following year with a cover version of Mambo No.5.

In each episode Bob and his friends work together on a project during which they highlight the importance of social skills, cooperation and morals.

Famous "guest appearances" on the show have included Sue Barker, Chris Evans, Noddy Holder, Elton John, Ulrika Jonsson and John Motson.

Bob the Builder

Fifi and the Flowertots

Keith saw a gap in the market for a television series aimed at pre-school girls, this lead to the creation of Fifi and the Flowertots. A group of flower based characters that have fun adventures in their garden.

The show was first broadcast in 2005 with actress Jane Horrocks supplying the voice of the main character Fifi Forget-me-not.

Fifi and the Flowertots followed in the footsteps of 'Bob' in becoming a worldwide success with the show being sold to over 140 territories.

Roary the Racing Car

Chapman Entertainment's latest creation, Roary, follows the adventures of a young racing car who lives at Silver Hatch racetrack.

The idea was developed after Keith was introduced to a man called David Jenkins who worked in the motor industry at Brands Hatch Race Circuit.

Comedian Peter Kay provides the voice of one of the main characters Big Chris, the karaoke loving mechanic with racing legend Sir Stirling Moss supplying the shows narrative.

The show looks well on its way to mimic the success of 'Bob' and 'Fifi' with the show being aired in over 20 countries worldwide with plans to launch elsewhere in the coming years.

Stuart Bingham

Professional Snooker player, Stuart Bingham is currently ranked at 21st by the World Snooker Association. The ranking system is calculated by a point system over a period of two years (2006/07 & 2007/08) from Stuart's performance in the later of those two years only 14 other players collected more points than he did.

Stuart already has his place in snooker history being the first player ever to win the Masters Qualifying Event twice. During his 2005 campaign Stuart scored his second maximum 147 break, the first being at the UK Tour Event (1999)

Stuarts other achievements to date include:
Reaching the Quarter Final of the Welsh Open in 1999, beating World Champion, John Higgins, in the Third round.
A shock 1st round victory over Stephen Hendry in the 2000 World Championship. Stuarts ranking at the time being just 97th in the world!
Reaching the Quarter-Finals of the Grand Prix tournament in 2005/6 season, once again beating a World Champion, Shaun Murray in the third round before going on to get beaten by the eventual tournament winner, John Higgins.
Yet another Quarter-Final finish, this time in the 2005 UK Championship.

The 2007/08 Shanghai Masters where Stuart competed in another Quarter-Final match up, this time being stopped by Mark Selby.

Stuart was born in Basildon on 21st May 1976; He attended Swan Mead Infant & Junior School (now called Cherry Tree Primary) and then Barstable School. As a child he lived at Pitseaville Grove in Vange where he spent a lot of his time playing football on the nearby field.

The Bingham family then moved to Hockley Road (off Long Riding). It is here where Stuart first started playing snooker. His brother and two mates used to play down the Commodore Pub at Stacey's Corner and one day Stuart tagged along to make up the pairs. It was there that he was spotted by the manager Dave Meads. Stuart says of the snooker club *"That's where I hung out for pretty much most of my childhood"*

Unfortunately the Commodore Public House and Snooker club are no longer there, having being knocked down and replaced by residential buildings.

Stuart also lived at Butneys, in Ghyllgrove before moving back to the Vange area where he now lives with his girlfriend Lyndsey.

Due to the nature of the sport, Stuart spends a lot of his time away competing in tournaments throughout the world.

"When I have been away at a tournament, it is always nice to come back to the familiar surroundings of Basildon, it is my home"

Eamonn Martin

Nicknamed the 'Lion of Laindon', Eamonn was born in Basildon on the 9th October 1958 and attended Fryerns Grammar School. At 16 years old he joined the Basildon Athletic Club, with whom he is still closely affiliated.

Eamonn represented Great Britain at three Olympic Games between 1984 and 1992, Los Angeles (5,000 metres), Seoul (5,000metres & 10,000metres) and Barcelona (10,000metres)

He also won a Gold medal in the 10,000 metres race at the 1990 Commonwealth Games held in Auckland, New Zealand.

However, it is his win at the 1993 London Marathon for which Eamonn is most famously remembered. He finished with a time of 2:10:50 and is the last British man to have won the event. Over recent years, the international runners - most notably the Kenyan athletes - have dominated the 26 miles long race, making it likely that Eamonn will hold this claim for many years to come.

In addition to his success in London, Eamonn went on to win the 1995 Chicago Marathon aged 37.

On the 7th January 1989 Eamonn officially opened the Markhams Chase Centre where a plaque commemorating his achievements remains on show.

Eamonn continues to live and work locally in Basildon.

James Tomkins

James was born in Basildon on March 29th 1989 and plays professional football in The Barclays Premier League for West Ham United.

He started with the club at a very young age and during the 2007/08 season broke into the first team with 5 Premiership starts, plus one appearance as a substitute, and was named "Young Hammer of the Year".

Seven days before his 19th birthday, James made his debut for the first team club in an away fixture at Everton. He played the full 90 minutes, successfully contributing to a match which ended as a 1-1 draw. He very nearly got his name on the score sheet after just four minutes when he headed a chance which ricocheted off the crossbar.

Over the years James has represented his country at U15, U16, U17. U19 and is currently part of the England U21 squad.

During the preparations for the European Under-19 Championships in 2008, James found time to attend and hand out the honours at the first 'Sports Awards Night' at Chalvedon School, Wickford Avenue, where he was once a pupil himself.

After a five week loan spell with Derby County, Tomkins was recalled into the West Ham squad by the clubs new manager Gianfranco Zola and has since become an important part of the Premiership sides' 1st team squad.

In April 2009, in front of his home crowd at The Boleyn Ground, James netted his debut goal for West Ham against Sunderland in the 2-0 victory.

Terry Marsh

Terry moved to Basildon as a child from Stepney, East London. Shortly after the move, Terry joined Blue House Amateur Boxing Club and had his first fight for the Basildon club against Mark Gibb (Southend). The local newspaper, *Evening Echo*, was there to record the fight and gave a glowing report.

Whilst still in his teens, Terry joined the Royal Marines. Terry had to make a decision between serving in the infamous 'bandit country', otherwise know as Crossmaglen, South Armagh in Northern Ireland, or trying to qualify to box at the Olympic Games in Moscow. At the time, he never saw himself as having a future in boxing, and so committed himself to what he considered to be 'real soldier' work and served in Northern Ireland for four months.

Terry knew that in order to move up the military ranks, he would need academic qualifications. So in order to finance his studies he accepted an offer to box professionally by promoter/manager Frank Warren. Terry enrolled himself at Basildon College (now Thurrock and Basildon College) and took five O levels in Maths, English, Physics, Electronics and Chemistry.

Terry won his first professional fight in Bloomsbury, London in 1981. After six rounds of boxing against Andrew De Costa he was awarded the fight on a points decision.

A few years later, Terry joined the local Fire Brigade, being assigned a post at Tilbury Fire Station. As a result, the boxing media were quick to give him the moniker "The Fighting Fireman".

It wasn't long before he earned a shot at the British Boxing Title against Clinton McKenzie in September, 1984. The fight, held at the Britannia Leisure Centre in Shoreditch, was settled after 12 rounds on a points decision. Terry was awarded the Lonsdale belt and became the new British Light-Welterweight Champion.

Terry's next major contest was against the Italian Alessandro Scapecchi in Monte Carlo. A ten-count knock down in the sixth round earned him the European Light-Welterweight title.

On March 4th 1987, Terry fought for the IBF World Light-Welterweight Title against Joe Manley (USA). The venue was Terry's home town of Basildon. There was no arena big enough to house such an event so Frank Warren arranged for a giant 'Super tent' to be erected in the car park of the Festival Hall on Pipps Hill Close (now part of the Festival Leisure Park). The demand for tickets was huge; such was the interest in this fight that they could have sold out a tent with twice the capacity. The nearby hotel was used as changing rooms and the fighters had to make their way from there to the tent on, what turned out to be, a bitterly cold night.

The atmosphere was electric, with the vocal crowd singing and chanting Terry's name throughout. Fast paced right from the start, Terry came out looking quick and confident. The pressure was put onto the American with a lot of up close and inside fighting. After some beautiful combination of punches, Terry pounded into Manley forcing him up against the ropes which in turn brought the crowd to their feet. Manley was not given an inch of room throughout the whole fight and just before the end of the 9th round, he was knocked to the ground and had to pull himself up for a standing eight count.

Going into the tenth, Terry threw a barrage of punches which led to Referee, Randy Neumann, stepping in and stopping the fight. Terry celebrated with a forward flip and was duly crowned the new IBF Light-Welterweight Champion of the World. Commentators for the ITN hailed it as *"one of the best British victories seen in a long time"*.

The following day, Terry returned to work at the Fire Station. The win had made Terry a national celebrity and offers of interviews and TV appearances came flooding in. He was also the subject of an episode of "This is Your Life" with Eamonn Andrews presenting him with the 'famous red book'.

Terry was asked to open the newly built leisure centre on Crest Avenue, Pitsea. The sports facility was, for 6 years, called 'The Terry Marsh Centre' until the Basildon District Council changed back to its original name, the Eversley Leisure Centre, in 1993. A mosaic of Terry was created to commemorate the opening and naming of the centre and can be found inside the reception foyer.

Terry had always been clear about his intentions, he had always aimed to win a world title, have one defence and then retire as the undefeated champion. The opportunity to achieve this presented itself after Terry defended his title against Japanese fighter Akio Kameda, at the Royal Albert Hall in Kensington. After the sixth round, Kameda collapsed on the ropes and the fight was over. However at this point, Terry didn't feel it an appropriate fight to retire on, due to its messy and untidy nature. Marsh was also keen to fight a flamboyant American fighter named Hector "Macho" Camacho who, ringside at the fight, declared that he wanted a shot at the title.

The decision was eventually taken out of his hands. A number of incidents over the previous couple of years made Terry concerned about his health, prompting him to make a visit to his GP. He was diagnosed with Epilepsy .This news was to have repercussions, not only on his boxing career, but also to his future in the Fire Service.

Terry eventually passed an MRI scan that allowed him to be issued with a new boxing licence. In the meantime, Terry had teamed up with Ambrose Mendy and Frank Maloney, working together as 'Mendy, Maloney and Marsh Promotions'.

It is during this time that Terry's ex manager and Promoter Frank Warren was shot outside a Barking theatre. There had been animosity between the two regarding a dispute over VAT payments owing to Terry,

Terry Marsh mosaic at Everley Leisure Centre

172

dating back to the World Title fight in Basildon, and a libel writ which had been issued by Warren over comments said by Terry during a TV interview.

Terry was not initially a suspect in the shooting and claimed to have been in the Strings Bar, Basildon with his brother John and an old acquaintance Mark Evans, when they heard the news about the attempt on Warren's life.

Upon returning to the UK, after attending a Nigel Benn fight in Atlanta City, Terry was arrested for the attempted murder of Frank Warren.

After spending a total of 10 months between Wormwood Scrubs, Pentonville and Brixton Prisons, Terry was finally released after a jury found him not guilty.

During his time on remand, Terry became somewhat of an expert on libel law *"I went to prison for those ten months because of libel laws, so I had time to learn a lot about it. When I got out I sued paper after paper for all the things alleged against me. I actually made more money out of libel than I did out of boxing"*

Terry decided to settle some old scores, namely the libel case against him by Frank Warren. The judge at the case made the comment that it was the first time that he had come across a defendant who was pushing for the commencement of an action.

Frank lost the case, which did not necessary mean that Terry had won, just that he had held his own – such is the nature of libel cases.

Terry tried his hand at acting and in 1989 he played the part of Curly in a film called Tank Malling starring Ray Winstone. Terry also played a character called Larry Cotton in an episode of Silent Witness named *Blood, Sweat and Tears*.

Terry also ran as the Liberal Democrat parliamentary candidate for the Basildon seat at the 1997 General Elections. An accusation was made against him of fraud and deception, he was later cleared of any charges, but the damage to his reputation forced him to bring political career to an abrupt end.

To add a further string to Terry's bow, he became a writer and a publisher in 2005. He released his autobiography "*Undefeated*" giving a detailed account of his childhood, boxing career, time in prison and his subsequent release. As part of the promotion for the book Terry recorded a song, accompanied by a music video, called 'Phil and Grant', a humorous tribute to the 'Mitchell brothers' from the TV soap opera Eastenders.

Terry now works in London's Finance sector and has done so for several years now, he still commutes to the city daily from his Basildon home.

Terry is currently raising awareness for his new political party/movement – Nota – which stands for "None of the above"

The plan is to field a Nota candidate in every constituency in the country, giving people the chance to vote for none of the above, as a means of registering and accurately recording voters' active abstention.

Nota's only policy is that if they are elected, they will immediately stand down thus forcing another by-election.

Joan Sims

One of Britain's much loved actresses; Joan was born on 9th May 1930 in Laindon, which back in those days would have been just a small village. Her father was the Station master at Laindon Train Station where Joan grew up.

There were very few children around for Joan to play with so she kept herself entertained by putting on little performances for the commuters at the station. Using the loading bay in the goods yard as her stage she would dress up in her mother's clothes and sing and dance for the people as they passed through the station.

Joan was sent by her parents to the private school, St Johns, in Billericay. She then went on to attend Brentwood High School for Girls.

Most Saturday mornings, Joan would go to the Radion Cinema on Laindon High Road where she would watch her hero's and heroines on the big screen, it is here that her dream to become an actress began to grow. Shortly after the war ended Joan joined the amateur dramatics club 'Langdon Players' and the local operatic society.

Joan was eventually accepted into the Royal Academy of Dramatic Arts (RADA) in London, graduating in 1950, aged 19. Joan signs up with a young up and coming theatrical agent called Peter Eade and her professional acting career begins.

Joan started out in repertory theatre, pantomime and revue performances before taking her first TV role providing the voices for a children's puppet show called 'Vegetable Village' (Joan played 3 characters - Millicent Mushroom, Barbara Beetroot and Oscar Onion)

Joan's first "official" feature film was 'Colonel March Investigates' made from a collection of TV episodes grouped together and released in 1952. Joan played the part of Marjorie Dawson, the secretary of the Colonel (played by Boris Karloff)

Her first "proper" film was to be one year later in a comedy starring George Cole, William Hartnell and John Pertwee called 'Will any Gentleman?' This would also be the first time Joan would work with the South African "Carry On" legend, Sid James.

Joan was offered a small part in the 'Doctor in the House' the first of the 6 'Doctor' films, playing the part of Nurse Rigor Mortis alongside Dirk Bogarde. The film went onto become a big hit at the box office and was quickly followed up by the sequel 'Doctor at Sea' where Joan's character, Wendy, finds herself competing for the love of the handsome young doctor with a young French singer played by Bridget Bardot, who was appearing for the first time in an English speaking film.

Joan went on to do two more 'Doctor' films - Doctor in Clover (1965) and Doctor in Trouble (1970).

In August 1958 Carry on Sergeant was released and proved a big success at the box office. Joan was contacted during the planning of the sequel and was asked if she was available. In November 1958 Joan went along to Pinewood Studios and started filming the first of her 24 appearances in the Carry On series. The film went on to become Britain's biggest box office hit that year, and also achieved much success in the US.

Appearing in 24 'Carry On' films made Joan the longest serving female member of the team and for each of those releases Joan was paid £2,500, half of what the male characters were earning. Inflation was never taken into consideration, with the same fee being given in 1958 as it was 20 years later. There were technicians in the crew that were earning more money than the actors, and no royalties were given to the cast members meaning they make nothing from the endless re-runs and compilation releases.

During the height of Joan's 'Carry On' fame she was invited to open the 'Garden Fete' in Laindon where she was expected to make a speech. Joan described it as being one of the most terrifying experiences of her acting life!

Joan made regular appearances in the TV series' 'As Time Goes By' (1994-1998) and 'On the Up' (1990-1992) 'Farrington of the F.O.' (1986-1987) plus the occasional part in TV shows 'Till death do us part', 'The Victoria Wood Show', 'The Goodies', 'The Two Ronnies', 'Doctor Who' and 'Only Fools and Horses'. Joan was also the female support on both 'The Dick Emery Show' and 'The Kenneth Williams Show' and was involved in several TV films including 'Love Among the Ruins' (1975) directed by George Cukor and starring Lawrence Olivier and Katherine Hepburn. *"Mine was a small role, but to be in the company of Olivier, Hepburn and Cukor made 'Love Among the Ruins' to be one of the high points of my whole career"*

Joan's professional life may have been filled with much laughter and joy but certain parts of her private life would prove to be anything but. A series of deaths to the people closest to Joan in the early 80's (including the passing of Hattie Jacques and her mother, Gladys Sims) lead her to start drinking heavily. Joan began to suffer from Depression and in 1982 was admitted into Banstead Hospital in Surrey. A place which Joan herself described as being *"where people go to when they can't afford the Priory"*

Joan suffered with depression many times throughout her life and in 1999 Joan was diagnosed as having Bells Palsy, *a symptom of which where one side of the face becomes paralysed.* Unable to get work with this condition Joan reacted by hitting the bottle. Joan was luckily able to pull herself back together again and landed a part in a TV Film called 'The Last Blonde Bombshell' featuring an all star cast of Dame Judy Dench, Dame Cleo Laime, Sir Ian Holme, June Whitfield and Leslie Caron.

Unfortunately this became Joan's last work, a fall left her with a fractured hip, which she had replaced, but complications during a later routine operation caused her to slip into a coma. Joan died on the 28th June 2001 aged 71. She was cremated at Putney Cemetery where her ashes were scattered in the grounds.

Before she died, Joan released her autobiography "High Spirits" the title taken from one of her favourite revues of the 1950s and in 2002 the documentary 'The Unforgettable Joan Sims' was released on ITV.

There are two plagues dedicated to the memory of the much loved actress, the first was unveiled by her 'Carry On' co-star Barbara Windsor on 29th September 2002 at the flat where she lived in Thackeray Street, Kensington, London. The second was unveiled on 9th May 2005 at Laindon Train Station by the Joan Sims Appreciation Society.

Plaque at Laindon train station

Denise Van Outen

Denise was born in Basildon Hospital, but lived in nearby Corringham / Stanford-le-Hope. She attended the Sylvia Young Theatre School in London and is often referred to as the 'Basildon Babe' by the national media.

Denise shot to fame in 1997 alongside Johnny Vaughan presenting 'The Big Breakfast' on Channel 4. In 1998 the pair released a cover version of Kylie Minogue & Jason Donovan's single "Especially for You" which reached No.3 in the UK charts.

Her big break lead to a series of acting, presenting and radio jobs, however, Denise became almost as well known for her personal life as she was for her professional career. She has famously dated public figures such as Gary Glitter (Glam rock singer), Andy Miller (guitarist from Dodgy), Jay Kay (singer of Jamiroquai) and most recently Lee Mead (winner of the 2007 TV talent show 'Any Dream Will Do') to whom she married in April 2009.

Throughout her career, Denise has been closely linked to the theatre having performed in some of the worlds most renowned and respected productions.

At the age of eleven Denise played the character of Eponine in the World's longest running musical, Les Miserables.

Denise played the lead role, Roxie Hart, in the hit musical Chicago at the Adelphi Theatre, London in 2001. She later went on to play the same role on Broadway in New York.

Andrew Lloyd Webber's remake of the musical 'Tell Me on a Sunday' in 2003 saw Denise tread the boards once again in a solo show, specially re-written just for her. The show ran for ten months in the West End before embarking on a nationwide tour the following year.

In Jonathan Larson's new version of the stage show Rent in October 2007, Denise returned to the West End playing the part of bi-sexual performance artist Maureen.

Denise teamed up with Andrew Lloyd Webber again as a judge on the BBC 1 reality show 'Any Dream Will Do!'. A show which had the task of casting the next leading man for 'Joseph and the Amazing Technicolor Dreamcoat'

She was then a judge on the stateside version of the musical reality show 'Grease: You're the One that I Want' which found new talent to play the parts of Sandy and Danny.

In 2008 the programme was back with a new objective and a new title 'I'd Do Anything'. Denise was once again part of the judging panel which found performers to play 'Oliver' and 'Nancy' for the West End hit musical 'Oliver'

Scott Robinson

Scott attended Eversley Primary School in Pitsea, followed by Chalvedon Comprehensive School, before joining the Sylvia Young Theatre School in year 9.

He made TV appearances on Casualty, Hale & Pace and The Bill before achieving international success with pop band 'FIVE'.

FIVE sold over 20 million records worldwide between 1997 and 2001, with 12 top ten singles and 4 top ten albums. Their hits included "Slam Dunk Da Funk" "When the Lights Go Out" "Got the Feeling" "Everybody Get Up" "Keep on Movin'" "We Will Rock You" and "Let's Dance".

The group picked up a BRIT Award for Best Pop Act in 2000 and The MTV Select Award at the MTV Europe Music Awards in 1998.

Shortly after the band split in 2001 Scott became friends with DJ Chris Brooks whilst working on local radio station Essex FM. Together they started a management company called 'Killer Media'

Scott has since toured with the musical Boogie Nights 2 and runs his own shop in Leigh on Sea called 'Celebrity Scribbles' - an autograph and memorabilia store.

Jillean Hipsey

Jillean captained the England Netball team from 1980 - 87, playing in three 'World Games'.

Jillean grew up in Laindon and Langdon Hill, attending Markhams Chase School (now Janet Duke) before going onto Fryerns Grammar. It was at school where Jillean first started playing Netball.

At the Seventh World Tournament, held in Glasgow, Jillean received her 100th playing cap for her country and in doing so earned herself a place in the Guinness Book of Records, as the first English player to reach the century mark. England went on to finish 4th in the competition behind New Zealand, Australia and Trinidad.

Jillean now lives in Maylandsea, Essex and still plays netball for New Cambell Netball Club in the Essex Met League.

"I consider myself fortunate that I have played for good clubs and a good county which led me to be picked for England. My club in Basildon was Laindon, formed by Chris Laundy a founder member of the Basildon District netball league. This was a very pro-active and far sighted league. It was a great start for me as from there I went to Cambell, then county and England."

"There is nothing as good as standing up to the National Anthem representing your country. Even now, the Anthem still sends shivers up my spine! It is a great honour and privilege to represent your country at any sport. It takes dedication and hard work, but along the way, you make many friends with a common interest."

Brian Belo

In 2007 the notorious 'reality TV show' Big Brother was won by Basildon boy Brian Belo. The 19 year old from Ampers End was working as a data entry clerk before entering the infamous house. Fourteen weeks later and with 60.3% of the final votes he is crowned as the overall winner of Big Brother 8, taking home £100,000 in prize money.

Brian attended Bromfords School in Wickford, the same school as Chantelle Houghton, the winner of Celebrity Big Brother in 2006.

Brian enjoyed National publicity immediately after leaving the Big Brother house, accepting the many requests of TV guest appearances and showbiz party invites. Brian was given a guest spot on Harry Hill's TV Burps and a part as an extra in his favourite TV show Hollyoaks.

Back in Basildon, Brian was reaping the benefits of his new found fame and was 'handed the keys to Bas Vegas' at a ceremony organised by Jumpin Jaks at the Festival Leisure Park. Brian was given the red carpet treatment after arriving in a limo with a group of friends. Inside the club a special reserved VIP area was designated for Brian and his 'entourage' to enjoy.

In 2008 Brian released a music single named 'Essex Boy' which features the line "Oi yoghurt top, stop drinking that alcopop". The song was performed by Brian for the first time in front of an audience at the Sky Bar, Festival Leisure Park.

Since winning the show, Brian has also been involved in promoting 'The Essex County Councils Foster Care Awareness Fortnight' A campaign he is proud to be a part of having spent a brief spell as a foster child himself when he was younger.

Luke Biggins

Luke is an award winning music video director, producer and writer and has made quite a name for himself in the UK Hip Hop scene.

Luke attended St Anne Line Infant and Junior school, followed by St Anselms (now De la Salle), then onto South East Essex College and finally Staffordshire University, where he studied Film Production.

He started his career as a cameraman for film and TV, before moving into producing music videos and then later directing. He is now a well established director having won the 'Best of British (video) Channel U Award 2005' 'Barcelona Film Festival Award 2004' and the 'Soho broadcast Award, Promo Section 2004'

Over the years Luke has directed videos for many rock, pop and hip hop artists including – Bloc Party, Lilly Allen, Daniel Bedingfield, Keisha White, Hinda Hicks, Sway, Choong Family, Darren B, Aslan - Black Magician, T2, JMC and Black Twang. He also worked with Ludacris and the AllSaints to create videos for '3 Front Room'

In addition to music video's Luke has also directed several TV commercials, most notably the Renault Clio Sport 197 / Viral Campaign.

Together with MOBO award winning hip hop artist 'Black Twang', Luke is co-owner of Rotton Products and makes regular appearances on MTV Base.

Filming for Luke's first feature film 'The Block' is set to start at the end of 2009. Telling the story of a 24hr period set inside a London tower block, it is to be both written and directed by Luke.

Basildon: in the Media

Film

In the Richard Curtis film 'Love Actually', one character - Colin Frissell (played by Kris Marshall), goes to America convinced that his British accent will lead to the opposite sex falling for him. In the scene where he first comes in contact with a group of attractive young American girls (Elisha Cuthbert, Ivana Milicevic, January Jones, Shannon Elizabeth) he reveals to them that he is from 'Basildon' which causes the girls to swoon.

The movie 'Boston Kickout' (1995) starring John Simm (Life on Mars, The Lakes, Human Traffic), Andrew Lincoln (Love Actually, This Life, Teachers) and Marc Warren (Hustle, Green Street Hooligans, The Vice) is set in the original Newtown of Stevenage with the filming location being switched to Basildon close to the end of production. Director, Paul Hills, claimed that the local council tried to stop the film being made by banning the crew from semi public area's accusing the film makers of projecting a negative portrayal of Stevenage.

In a car crash scene, filmed in Basildon Town Centre, you can see signs of Basildon in the early 90's, with clear shots of the old Library (where Westgate Park now stands) and the row of shops on the Town Square, most of which have since changed. Also the clock tower is still prominent in the centre of the square, with the escalators leading up to High Pavement missing.

Television

Basildon was often mentioned in the BBC sit-com 'On the Buses' with one character, Iris being from the town. The show was set in the fictitious Essex town of 'Luxton' and in one episode, aired in 1973, a football match organised by conductor Blakey, sees the 'On the Buses' team 'The Luxton Lions' matched up against an all female team called 'The Basildon Bashers'.

Award winning British Comedy, 'Gavin and Stacey' was set in the Basildon District town of Billericay. Although very little filming was done in the area, as most of the shooting took place in Wales.

The show tells the story of an Essex Boy, Gavin Shipman (Matthew Horne) and Welsh girl, Stacey West (Joanna Page) falling in love, and the comedic intertwining of the couples eccentric and unconventional families and friends.

Writers Ruth Jones and James Corden, who also feature in the show as characters Ness and Smithy, have announced that there is to be a third series due for release later this year.

The Newtown gets a mention in the series by the Shipman's family friend, Damn Sutcliffe (Julia Davis) *"Sex-wise we were at an all time low. We were in a car park in Basildon the other night, flashing the headlights, no-one came. I just wanna feel involved"*

The 2004 ITV drama, 'Cant Buy Me Love' starring Martin Kemp and Michelle Collins, tells the story of a painter and decorator from Basildon who pretends to have won the lottery in an attempt to stop his wife leaving him.

The Channel Five series 'Police Interceptors' follows three 'intercept teams' around Basildon, Colchester and Chigwell. The documentary shows the newly formed police units, which use cutting edge technology and specially trained officers to arrest the most difficult-to-catch criminals in Britain.

Other...

Russell Brand makes reference to Basildon in his autobiography titled, My Booky Wook. The controversial comedian was born and raised in nearby Grays, Thurrock.

The internet video phenomenon 'Old Man Stan' takes a comical look at Basildon through the eyes of 'a local puppet pensioner'. The content of these hilarious music video's, all of which were filmed locally, are specifically Basildon related. With a collection of songs such as 'Fairy Tale of Basildon', 'Hit Me With Your Bazzo Stick' and 'Everyone's Gone To The Moon (on the Square)'

The growing popularity of Steve Waters' creation has taken Basildon by storm, with Old Man Stan featuring on the front page of local newspapers and each video having clocked up ten of thousands of online hits.

The amusing video's can be seen on Steve's website www.oldmanstan.co.uk or on www.youtube.com

In UK politics, Basildon is renowned for forecasting the overall result of a General Election, and has done so in every election since 1974. This is why the Basildon constituency is often described as a 'barometer' for election outcomes, and why it is watched closely on election nights by the media and indeed by some anxious political advisors.

The Festival Hall, at the site of the Festival Leisure Park (aka Bas Vegas), was, between 1985 and 1996, a top boxing venue. Many big names have fought there over the years, including Joe Calzaghe (WBO, IBF, WBA, WBC Super Middleweight champion and RING Light Heavyweight champion) Carl Thompson (WBO Cruiserweight champion 97-99) and Chris Eubank (WBO Middleweight and Super Middleweight champion).

Terry Marsh won his world title at the specially erected Super Tent in the grounds of the Festival Hall, also on the bill that night was Nigel Benn, who later went on to become both WBC Middleweight and Super Middleweight champion.

Bibliography

A Century of Basildon, Marion Hill, Sutton Publishing
Basildon, Peter Lucas, Phillimore & Co. Ltd
Basildon, A History & Celebration, Mara Cottrell, Francis Firth Collection
Basildon: A Pictorial History, Jessie K. Payne, Phillimore & Co Ltd
Basildon: Behind the Headlines, Peter Lucas
Basildon: Birth of a City, Peter Lucas
Basildon, Our Heritage, Frances Clamp, The History Press Ltd
Basildon Park: Berkshire, The National Trust
Basildon Plotlands, Deanna Walker, Phillimore & Co. Ltd
Brink of Despair, George Ross
Depeche Mode: Stripped, Jonathon Miller, Omnibus Press
Essex Place Names, James Kemble, Historical Publications Ltd
Ted Haley Recordings, stored in Essex Records Office, dated 1967
High Spirits, Joan Sims, Partridge (Division of Transworld Publishers)
History of Basildon, Billericay & Wickford, Basildon Council
Memories of Basildon, Jim Reeve, Tempus Publishing Ltd
The Place Names of Essex, P H Reaney, Cambridge University Press
Undefeated, Terry Marsh, Terry Marsh Publishing
Wendy Taylor, Edward Lucie-Smith, Art Books International
When Basildon was Farms and Fields, Jessie K Payne, Ian Henry Publications
www.Basildon.com